CUTE AND EASY
Crocheted
Baby Clothes

CUTE AND EASY

Crocheted
Baby Clothes

35 ADORABLE PROJECTS FOR 0–3 YEAR OLDS

Nicki Trench

CICO BOOKS
LONDON NEW YORK

Published in 2012 by CICO Books
an imprint of Ryland Peters & Small Ltd
20–21 Jockey's Fields, London WC1R 4BW

www.cicobooks.com

10 9 8 7 6 5 4 3 2 1

A CIP catalogue record for this book is
available from the British Library.

ISBN: 978 1 908170 29 3

Printed in China

Editor: Marie Clayton
Designer: Elizabeth Healey
Photographer: Penny Wincer
Stylist: Luis Peral-Aranda
Techniques illustrators: Kate Simunek
and Stephen Dew

For digital editions, visit
www.cicobooks.com/apps.php

Contents

→ Introduction   6

Techniques   8

CHAPTER 1
Jumpers and cardigans   16
→ Springtime jumper   18
→ Wrapover cardigan   22
→ Simple stripy tank top   26
→ Baby shell cardigan   28
→ Pocket trim cardigan   32
→ Flower power cardigan   36
→ Ship ahoy jumper   38
→ Heart tank top   40
→ Pompom cardigan   42
→ Frill-edged cardigan   44
→ Strawberry kisses jumper   48

CHAPTER 2
Stepping out   54
→ Lilac bootees   56
→ Ribbon hat   58
→ Beanie hat   60
→ Brimmed baby hat   62
→ Ophelia buggy blanket   64
→ Baby mittens   66
→ Sweetheart blanket   68
→ Pompom hat   70
→ Flower bonnet   72
→ Star stitch bootees   74
→ Flower cot blanket   76

CHAPTER 3
Jackets, shawls and dresses   78
→ Hooded jacket   80
→ Poncho   84
→ Tasselled baby poncho   88

→ Blossom shawl   90
→ Toggle jacket   92
→ Petal cape   96
→ Pink baby dress   100
→ Toddler dress   102

CHAPTER 4
**Toys, accessories and
room decorations**   106
→ Honey bunny   108
→ Coat hangers   112
→ Happy stars cot garland   116
→ Baby cloths   118
→ Billy the bear   122

→ Suppliers   126
→ Index   127
→ Acknowledgements   128

Introduction

There's an abundance of crochet in stores at the moment, so why not make your baby trendy, too? In this book we have brought you a range of baby clothes and accessories designed to delight. It doesn't matter if you're experienced or a beginner, there are projects to suit all and we've marked levels on each pattern so you can see which one suits your ability best: Beginner, Improver or Enthusiast.

Many of the designs have been influenced by vintage patterns and, in particular, those belonging to my mother that she made when I was a child. If you've been put off by old-fashioned baby bonnets made in yarn that would either make your baby's hair stand on end or come out in a rash, think again. Our contemporary versions will have you eagerly heading to your yarn store or internet supplier.

We've chosen really pretty colours to show off the projects and embellished them with tiny flowers, embroidery or ribbons. You don't have to stick with the traditional blue for boy and pink for girl theme; feel free to experiment with the delicious colours available.

I've mostly used the brand 'Rooster Yarns' for the projects, simply because it's great to crochet with. It is made from a mix of baby alpaca and merino wool and is supersoft against the baby's skin. It's also 100% natural, allowing the yarn to 'breathe' in the summer and still keep the baby warm in the winter. If you're substituting this yarn for something else, make sure you use a really soft yarn for delicate baby skins and where possible use wool rather than acrylic.

Many people are thrown into a panic by crochet patterns. This is a big part of learning to crochet. I still have a pencil next to me when I'm crocheting and mark off every row, even every stitch if it's a new technique I'm just learning. Follow the pattern row by row exactly and you won't go wrong. We have a Techniques section in the book too, with clear illustrations that will help you out of a tight spot if you need to learn something new, or just need a reminder.

Most of the garments in the book come in different sizes and the patterns can have lots of numbers in them. It's essential that before you start your pattern you go through and circle the size that you're following. It's always best to read a pattern before you start – it makes good bedtime reading instead of that dull old romantic novel!

Making things for a baby is completely satisfying, whether you're crocheting for your own baby as you sit anticipating its birth, or making a gift for family or friends. Most of the projects in this book are small and quick, or try one of the blankets or shawls – they could take the whole nine months!

Techniques

In this section, we explain how to master the simple crochet techniques that you need to make the projects in this book.

Making a slip knot
The simplest way is to make a circle with the yarn, so that the loop is facing downwards.

1 In one hand hold the circle at the top, where the yarn crosses, and let the tail drop down so that it falls in the centre of the loop. With your free hand or the tip of a crochet hook, pull the tail through the loop and pull the knot, so that it tightens loosely.

2 Put the hook into the circle and pull the knot gently so that it forms a loose loop on the hook.

Holding the hook
Pick up your hook as though you were picking up a pen or pencil. Keeping the hook held loosely between your fingers and thumb, turn your hand so that the palm is facing up and the hook is balanced in your hand and resting in the space between your index finger and your thumb.

Holding yarn

Pick up the yarn with your little finger in the opposite hand to your hook, with your palm facing upwards. Turn your hand to face downwards, with the yarn on top of your index finger and under the other two fingers and wrapped right around the little finger. Keeping your index finger only at a slight curve, hold your work just under the slip knot with the other hand.

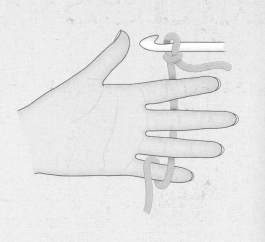

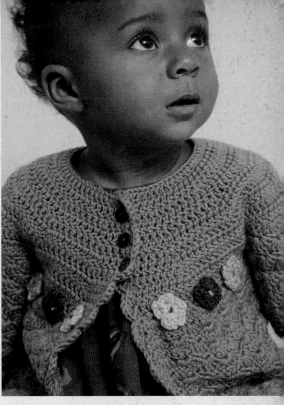

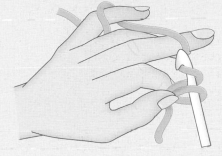

Yarn around hook

To create a stitch, you'll need to catch the yarn with the hook and pull it through the loop. Holding your yarn and hook correctly, catch the yarn from behind with the hook pointed upwards. As you gently pull the yarn through the loop on the hook, turn the hook so that it faces downwards and slide the yarn through the loop. The loop on the hook should be kept loose enough so that the hook slides through easily.

Chain

1 Using the hook, wrap the yarn around the hook and pull it through the loop on the hook, creating a new loop on the hook. Continue in this way to create a chain of the required length.

2 Keep moving your middle finger and thumb close to the hook, to hold the work in place with the opposite hand that you hold your hook with.

Chain ring/circle

If you are crocheting a round shape, one way of starting off is by crocheting a number of chains following the instructions in your pattern, and then joining them into a circle.

1 To join the chain into a circle, insert the crochet hook into the first chain that you made (not into the slip knot), yarn around hook, then pull the yarn through the chain and through the loop on your hook at the same time, thereby creating a slip stitch and forming a circle.

2 You will now have a circle ready according to your pattern.

Some of the circles in this book have been made by creating a spiral, whereby you make two chains and insert your hook into the second chain from the hook (the first chain you made). Following the instructions in the pattern will then ensure the spiral has the correct amount of stitches. It's essential to use a stitch marker when using this method, so that you know where to start and finish your round.

Marking rounds

Place a stitch marker at the beginning of each round; a piece of yarn in a contrasting colour is useful for this. Loop the stitch marker into the first stitch; when you have made a round and reached the point where the stitch marker is, work this stitch, take out the stitch marker from the previous round and put it back into the first stitch of the new round.

Joining new yarn

If using double crochet, insert the hook as normal into the stitch, using the original yarn, and pull a loop through. Drop the old yarn and pick up the new yarn. Wrap the new yarn around the hook and pull it through the two loops on the hook.

Slip stitch

A slip stitch doesn't create any height and is often used as the last stitch to create a smooth and even round or row.

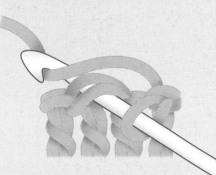

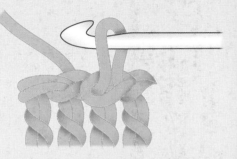

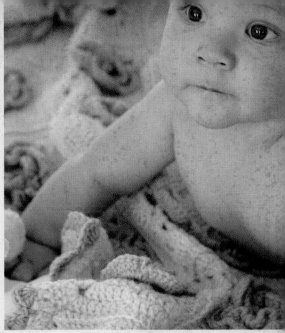

1 To make a slip stitch: put the hook through the work, yarn around hook.

2 Pull the yarn through both the work and through the loop on the hook at the same time.

Double crochet

1 Insert the hook into your work, yarn around hook and pull the yarn through the work. You will then have two loops on the hook.

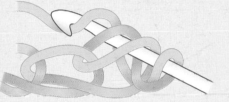

2 Yarn around hook again and pull through the two loops on the hook. You will then have one loop on the hook.

Half treble

1 Before inserting the hook into the work, wrap the yarn around the hook and put the hook through the work with the yarn wrapped around.

2 Yarn around hook again and pull through the first loop on the hook (you now have three loops on the hook).

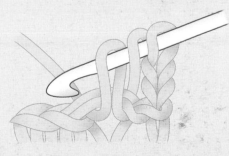

3 Yarn around hook and pull the yarn through all three loops. You'll be left with one loop on the hook.

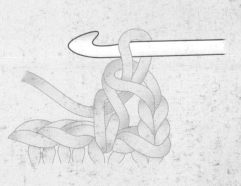

Treble

 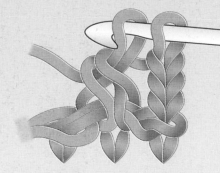 

1 Before inserting the hook into the work, wrap the yarn around the hook and put the hook through the work with the yarn wrapped around.

2 Yarn around hook again and pull through the first loop on the hook (you now have three loops on the hook). Yarn around hook again, pull the yarn through two loops (you now have two loops on the hook).

3 Pull the yarn through two loops again. You will be left with one loop on the hook.

Double treble

Yarn around hook twice, insert hook into the stitch, yarn around hook, pull a loop through (four loops on hook), yarn around hook, pull the yarn through two stitches (three loops on hook), yarn around hook, pull a loop through the next two stitches (two loops on hook), yarn around hook, pull a loop through the last two stitches.

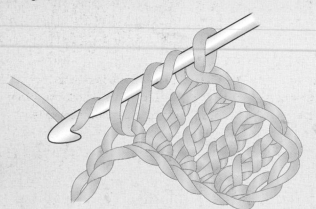

Triple treble

Yarn around hook three times, insert hook into the stitch, yarn around hook, pull a loop through (five loops on hook), yarn around hook, pull the yarn through two stitches (four loops on hook), yarn around hook, pull a loop through the next two stitches (three loops on hook), yarn around hook, pull a loop through the next two stitches (two loops on hook), yarn around hook, pull a loop through the last two stitches.

Quadruple treble

For quadtr, begin by wrapping the yarn around the hook four times and then proceed in the same way as for Triple Treble until you are left with one loop on the hook.

Loop stitch

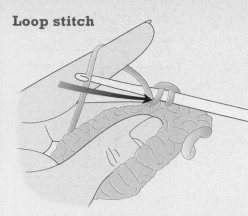 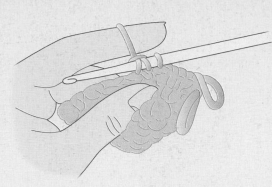 

1 With the yarn over the left index finger, insert the hook into the next stitch and draw two strands through the stitch (take the first strand from under the index finger and at the same time take the second strand from over the index finger).

2 Pull the yarn to tighten the loop, forming a 2.5cm (1in) loop on the index finger. Remove finger from the loop, put the loop to the back of the work, yarn around hook and pull through three loops on the hook (1 loop stitch made on right side of work).

Making rows

A turning chain is needed at the end of a row to create the height for the stitch, as follows:

Double crochet = 1 chain
Half treble crochet = 2 chain
Treble crochet = 3 chain
Double treble crochet = 4 chain
Triple treble crochet = 5 chain
Quadruple treble crochet = 6 chain

Intarsia

Use small balls of wool; one each side of the motif, and one or more for the motif. Use the background colour to one stitch before the motif; change colour by bringing in the motif colour on the last pull through of the stitch. Crochet the motif stitch(es) as per the chart; one stitch before the end of the motif change to the background colour in the same way. Keep colour changes to the WS of the work.

Chain space

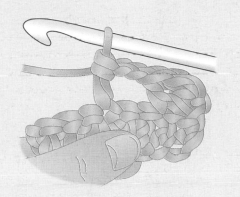 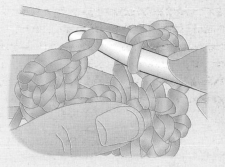

1 A chain space (ch sp) is the space that has been made under a chain in the previous round or row, and falls in between other stitches.

2 Stitches into a chain space are made directly into the hole created under the chain and not into the chain stitches themselves.

Decreasing

You can decease by either missing the next stitch and continuing to crochet, or by crocheting two or more stitches together. The basic technique is the same no matter which stitch you are using; the illustration shows working three trebles (tr3tog) in progress:

Work a treble into each of the next three stitches as normal, but leave the last loop of each stitch on the hook (four loops on the hook). Yarn around hook and pull the yarn through all the stitches on the hook to join them together. You will finish with one loop on the hook.

Increasing

Make two or three stitches into one stitch from the previous row. The illustration shows a two-stitch increase being made.

Double crochet two stitches together

1 Insert hook into next stitch, draw a loop through, insert hook into next stitch.

2 Draw a loop through, yarn around hook and pull through all three stitches.

Half treble two stitches together

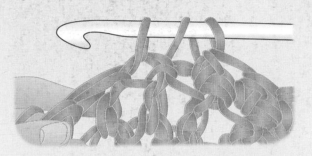

1 Yarn around hook, insert hook into next stitch, yarn around hook, draw yarn through (three loops on hook).

2 Yarn around hook, insert hook into next stitch, yarn around hook, draw yarn through.

3 Draw yarn through all five loops on hook.

Fastening off

Cut the yarn leaving a tail of approx 10cm (4in). Pull the tail all the way through the loop.

How to double crochet squares together

Place two squares wrong sides together, lining them up so that the stitches on each square match. Put the hook through the top loops of the first square and also through the corresponding top loops of the second square. Join in the yarn, make 1 chain, insert the hook into the top stitches of both squares and make a double crochet seam across the top of the squares.

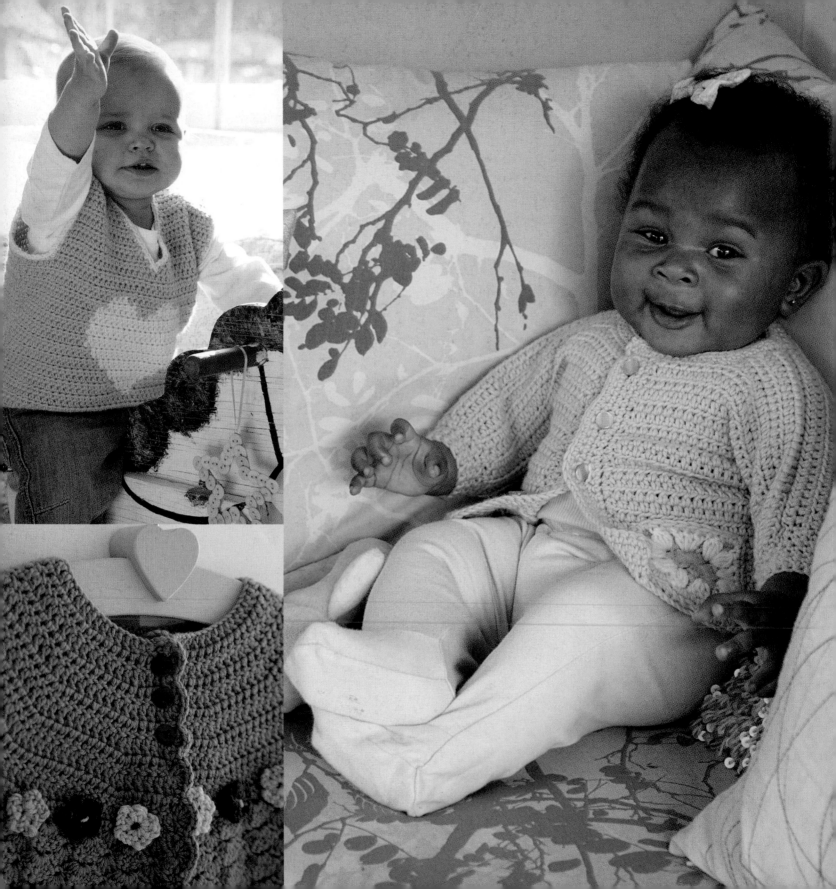

CHAPTER ONE

Jumpers and Cardigans

Springtime Jumper

A warm and cosy jumper suitable for girl or boy. The
squares, based on the traditional 'granny square',
are easy for beginners; it's in the 'Improver' category
only because of the picot and neck shaping.

Materials

Rooster Almerino DK

→ 3 x 50g (1¾oz) balls – approx 337.5m (372yds) – of shade
201 Cornish (off white) (MC)

→ 1 x 50g (1¾oz) ball – approx 112.5m (124yds) – each of
shade 203 Strawberry Cream (pale pink) (A), 209 Smoothie
(rust) (B), 205 Glace (pale blue) (C), 210 Custard (yellow)
(D), 207 Gooseberry (green) (E) and 204 Grape (purple)

→ 4mm (F/5) crochet hook

Abbreviations

ch chain; **ch sp** chain space; **dc** double crochet; **htr** half treble;
MC main colour; **rep** repeat; **RS** right side; **sp** space;
ss slip stitch; **st(s)** stitch(es); **tr** treble; **WS** wrong side;
yrh yarn round hook

Special abbreviations

htr2tog (half treble 2 together decrease) *yrh, insert hook in
next st, yrh, pull yarn through (3 loops on hook). Without
finishing st, rep from * in next st (5 loops on hook), yrh, pull yarn
through all 5 loops on hook

tr2tog (treble 2 together decrease) *yrh, insert hook in next st,
yrh, pull yarn through, yrh, pull yarn through 2 loops on hook (2
loops on hook). Without finishing st, rep from * in next st (3 loops
on hook), yrh, pull yarn through all 3 loops on hook

Size

To fit age: 12–24 months

Finished size

Chest: 57.5cm (23in)

Length: 32.5cm (13in)

Sleeve Seam: 19cm (7½in)

Tension

1 square measures approx 6cm (2.5in) using a 4mm (F/5) hook.
Sleeves: 20 sts x 14 rows over a 10cm (4in) square working half
treble using a 4mm (F/5) hook.

Square (make 30)

Use different colour combinations on each square; always use MC for Round 2.

Using first colour, make a loop, make 4ch, join with ss in first ch to form a ring.

Round 1: 3ch, 2tr in ring, 2ch, 3tr in ring, 2ch, *3tr in ring, 2ch; rep from * once more, ss in top of first 3ch.

  Fasten off.

  Put hook in any ch sp, join in MC.

Round 2: 3ch, 2tr, 3ch, 3tr in same ch sp (first corner), 2ch, *3tr, 3ch, 3tr in next ch sp, 2ch; rep from * twice more, ss in top of first 3ch.

  Fasten off.

  Put hook in top of fasten off st, join in third colour, make 1ch.

Round 3: 1dc in top of next 2 sts, 3dc in next ch sp, 1dc in top of next 3 sts, 2dc in next ch sp, *1dc in top of next 3 sts, 3dc in next ch sp, 1dc in top of next 3 sts, 2dc in next ch sp; rep from * twice more, ss in top of first ch.

  Fasten off.

  Sew in ends neatly and securely after making each square.

Back (16 squares)

Using dc seams, join strips of four squares across by four squares down to make a 16-square panel.

Front (14 squares)

Using dc seams, join together strips of four squares across by three squares down.

  To create hole for neck join one square on each outside strip (left and right of front).

Shoulders

Using MC and with RS facing, join yarn in top right-hand corner of front piece and work in tr as follows:

Row 1: 1ch, 1tr in each st across square.

Fasten off.

Row 2: Using A, join yarn at beginning (not end) of previous row in top of first 3-ch, 3ch, 1tr in each st across.

Fasten off.

Row 3: Using B, join yarn at beginning (not end) of previous row in top of first 3-ch, 3ch, 1tr in each st across.

Fasten off.

Rep on other shoulder, joining yarn and starting at top outside edge.

Joining shoulders:

Using a tapestry needle and suitable yarn colour, join shoulder seams.

Neck

Using MC and with RS facing, join MC in back of neck at right-hand side of jumper in corner st of shoulder and dc joining seam of square and work in htr as follows:

Row 1: 2ch, 1htr in each st across back (30 sts), 2htr in each colour (row end from shoulders, 6 sts), 1htr in each st down left front edge (11 sts), 1htr in corner seam st, 1htr in next and each st across centre front (27 sts), 1htr in corner seam st, 1htr in next and each st up right front (12 sts), 2htr in each colour (row end from shoulders), 1htr in corner seam (7 sts), join with ss in first 2-ch. (93 sts)

Join in B.

Row 2: 2ch, [1htr in each of next 8 sts, htr2tog] three times, 1htr in each of next 2 sts, htr2tog, 1htr in each of next 9 sts, htr2tog, [1htr in each of next 6 sts, htr2tog] four times, 1htr in each of next 9 sts, htr2tog, 1htr in next 2 sts, htr2tog, 1htr in shoulder seam, join with ss in top of first 2-ch. (83 sts)

Join in C.

Row 3: 2ch, [1htr in each of next 7 sts, htr2tog] three times, 1htr in next st, htr2tog, 1htr in each of next 8 sts, [tr2tog] four times, 1htr in each of next 6 sts, tr2tog, 1htr in each of next 6 sts, [tr2tog] four times, 1htr in each of next 7 sts, htr2tog, 1htr in each of next 2 sts, htr2tog, 1htr in next next st, join with ss in top of first 2-ch. (68 sts)

Join in A.

Row 4: 2ch, 1htr in each of next 5 sts, htr2tog, 1htr in each of next 7 sts, htr2tog, 1htr in each of next 7 sts, htr2tog, 1htr in each of next 7 sts, [tr2tog] three times, 1htr in each of next 5 sts, htr2tog, 1htr in each of next 6 sts, [tr2tog] three times, 1htr in each of next 7 sts, htr2tog, 1htr in each of next 3 sts, ss in top of first 2-ch.

Join in MC.

Row 5 (picot): *3ch, ss in same st, 3ch, ss in next st; rep from * to end.

Fasten off.

Sides

Left side (back):

With RS facing, join MC at side edge of back piece in second square down from shoulder and in centre stitch of square, 1ch, 1dc in each st to bottom edge.

Join in D.

Next row: 1dc in each st to end.

Fasten off.

Left side (front):

With RS facing, join MC in bottom corner st, 1ch, 1dc in each st to centre st of second square from shoulder.

Join in E.

Next row: 1dc in each st to end.

Fasten off.

Right side (back):

With RS facing, join MC at side edge in bottom corner st, 1ch, 1dc in each st to centre st of second square from shoulder.

Join in D.

Next row: 1dc in each st to end.

Fasten off.

Right side (front):

With RS facing, join in E at side edge of front piece, in second square down from shoulder and in centre st of square, 1ch, 1dc in each st to bottom edge.

Join in MC.

Next row: 1dc in each st to end.

Fasten off.

Bottom

Front:

With WS facing, join in D in left corner of bottom edge, 2ch, 1htr in each row end of side panel, 1htr in each st along bottom edge (of squares), 1htr in each row end of second side panel. Break yarn.

Join in C.

Next row: 2ch, 1htr in each st to end. Break yarn.

Join in B.

Next row: 2ch, 1htr in each st to end. Break yarn.

Join in MC.

Next row (picot): *3ch, 1ss in same st, 1ss in next st; rep from * to end.

Fasten off.

Rep for back.

With WS facing, join side panel seams.

Sleeves

With RS facing, join MC in underarm st at front.

Row 1: 2ch, using htr, make 48 sts evenly around sleeve edge (htr2tog in last sts if necessary to achieve 48 sts), turn.

Row 2: 2ch, 1htr in each st to end, ss in top of first 2-ch, turn.

Row 3: 2ch, 1htr in each st to end, ss in top of first 2-ch, turn.

Row 4: 2ch, 1htr in next st, htr2tog, 1htr in each st to last 3 sts, htr2tog, 1htr in last st, turn. (46 sts)

Row 5: Rep Row 4. (44 sts)

Row 6: Rep Row 4. (42 sts)

Row 7: Rep Row 4. (40 sts)

Row 8: 2ch, 1htr in each st to end, ss in top of first 2-ch, turn.

Row 9: Rep Row 8.

Row 10: Rep Row 4. (38 sts)

Row 11: Rep Row 8.

Row 12: Rep Row 2. — *miss out R12*

Row 13: Rep Row 4. (36 sts)

Rows 14–15: Rep Row 2. *miss Row 15*

Row 16: Rep Row 4. (34 sts)

Rows 17–18: Rep Row 2.

Row 19: Rep Row 4. (32 sts)

Rows 20–21: Rep Row 2.

Row 22: Rep Row 4. (30 sts). Break yarn.

Sleeve cuffs:

Join in D.

Row 1: 1ch, 1dc in first st, *dc2tog, 1dc in each of next 2 sts; rep from * to end, ss in first 1-ch. Break yarn.

Join in C.

Row 2: 1ch, 1dc in each st to end. Break yarn.

Join in B.

Row 3: Rep Row 2. Break yarn.

Join in A.

Row 4: Rep Row 2. Break yarn.

Join in MC.

Row 5: Ss in next st, *3ch, ss in same st, ss in next st; rep from * to end.

Fasten off.

Finishing

With WS facing, join sleeve seams. Sew in ends.

Wrapover Cardigan

A very pretty cardigan which is perfect

for growing babies as it wraps over

rounded tummies.

Materials

Rooster Almerino DK

➔ 2:**3**:3:**4** x 50g (1¾oz) balls – approx 225:**337.5**:337.5:**450**m
(248:**372**:372:**496**yds) – of shade 201 Cornish (off white) (A)

Rooster Almerino Baby

➔ 1 x 50g (1¾oz) ball – approx 125m (136.5yds) – of shade 505 Candy Floss
(pink) (B)

➔ 3mm (D/3) crochet hook

Abbreviations

ch chain; **dc** double crochet; **dc2tog** (double crochet 2 together decrease)
insert hook in next st, yrh, pull yarn through (2 loops on hook). Without
finishing st, insert hook in next st, yrh, pull yarn through (3 loops on hook),
yrh, pull yarn through all 3 loops on hook; **rep** repeat; **RS** right side; **ss** slip
stitch; **st(s)** stitch(es); **tr** treble; **yrh** yarn round hook

Special abbreviations

tr2tog (treble 2 together decrease) *yrh, insert hook in next st, yrh, pull yarn
through, yrh, pull yarn through 2 loops on hook (2 loops on hook). Without
finishing st, rep from * in next st (3 loops on hook), yrh, pull yarn through all 3
loops on hook

tr3tog (treble 3 together decrease) *yrh, insert hook in next st, yrh, pull yarn
through, yrh, pull yarn through 2 loops on hook (2 loops on hook). Without
finishing st, rep from * in each of next 2 sts (4 loops on hook), yrh, pull yarn
through all 4 loops on hook

Size

To fit age: 0–3:**3–6**:6–12:**12–18** months

Finished size

Chest	(cm):	44	**49**	54	**59**
	(in):	17¼	**19¼**	21½	**23½**
Length	(cm):	19	**20.5**	26.5	**29**
	(in):	7½	**8¼**	10½	**11½**
Sleeve seam	(cm):	12.5	**15.5**	19.5	**24**
	(in):	5	**6¼**	7¾	**9½**

Tension

18 sts x 10 rows over a 10cm (4in) square working treble using a 3mm
(D/3) hook.

Body

Using A, make 123:**140**:150:**167**ch.

Row 1: 1dc in second ch from hook, 1dc in each ch to end.

Rows 2–4: 3ch, 1tr in each st to end.
(122:**139**:149:**166** sts)

Shape front slopes:

Dc2tog twice at each end of next 4:**7**:8:**10** rows. (106:**111**:117:**126** sts)

Body should now measure approx 8:**10**:12.5:**14**cm (3¼:**4**:5:**5½**in).

Divide for armholes, first front:

Row 1: Tr3tog at front edge, 1tr in each of next 19:**21**:23:**26** sts, tr3tog at armhole edge, turn. (21:**23**:25:**28** sts)

Row 2: Tr2tog twice at armhole edge, 1tr in each st to last 4 sts, tr2tog twice at front edge. (17:**19**:21:**24** sts)

Row 3: Tr2tog twice at front edge, 1tr in each st to last 4 sts, tr2tog twice at armhole edge. (13:**15**:17:**20** sts)

Row 4: Tr2tog twice at front edge, 1tr in each st to end. (11:**13**:15:**18** sts)

Row 5: 1tr in each st to end. (11:**13**:15:**18** sts)

Row 6: 1tr in each st to last 4 sts, tr2tog twice. (9:**11**:13:**16** sts)

Rows 7–9: 1tr in each st to end. (9:**11**:13:**16** sts)

Row 10: 1tr in each st to last 2 sts, tr2tog. (8:**10**:12:**15** sts)

Size 0–3 months, fasten off.

Row 11: Tr2tog, 1tr in each st to end. (8:**9**:11:**14** sts)

Rows 12–13: 1tr in each st to end. (8:**9**:11:**14** sts)

Size **3–6** months, fasten off.

Row 14: 1tr in each st to last 2 sts, tr2tog. (8:**9**:10:**12** sts)

Size 6–12 months, fasten off.

Row 15: Tr2tog, 1tr in each st to end. (8:**9**:10:**11** sts)

Size **12–18** months, fasten off.

Shape back:

Return to last complete row worked of body before arm shaping.

Row 1: Miss 3 sts, join yarn to next st, tr3tog, 1tr in each of next 42:**45**:47:**50** sts, tr3tog, turn. (44:**47**:49:**52** sts)

Row 2: Tr2tog twice at each end of row. (40:**43**:45:**48** sts)

Row 3: Tr2tog twice at each end of row. (36:**39**:41:**44** sts)

Rows 4–10: 1tr in each st to end. (36:**39**:41:**44** sts)

Shape back, neck and shoulder:

1tr in each of next 7:**8**:9:**10** sts, tr3tog. (8:**9**:10:**11** sts)

Fasten off.

Return to last complete row worked of body before shaping back neck.

Miss next 16:**17**:17:**18** sts, join yarn to next st.

Tr3tog, 1tr in each st to end.

Fasten off.

Second front:

Return to last complete row worked of body before arm shaping.

Row 1: Miss 3 sts, tr3tog, 1tr in each of next 19:**21**:23:**26** sts, tr3tog. (21:**23**:25:**28** sts)

Row 2: 3ch, tr2tog twice, 1tr in each st to last 4 sts, tr2tog twice. (17:**19**:21:**24** sts)

Row 3: Tr2tog twice at armhole edge, 1tr in each st to last 4 sts, tr2tog twice. (13:**15**:17:**20** sts)

Row 4: Tr2tog twice at front edge. (11:**13**:15:**18** sts)

Row 5: 3ch, 1tr in each st to end. (11:**13**:15:**18** sts)

Row 6: Tr2tog twice, 1tr in each st to end. (9:**11**:13:**16** sts)

Rows 7–9: 1tr in each st to end. (9:**11**:13:**16** sts)

Row 10: Tr2tog, 1tr in each st to end. (8:**10**:12:**15** sts)

Size 0–3 months, fasten off.

Row 11: 1tr in each st to last 3 sts, tr2tog. (8:**9**:11:**14** sts)

Rows 12–13: 1tr in each st to end. (8:**9**:11:**14** sts)

Size **3–6** months, fasten off.

Rows 14: Tr2tog, 1tr in each st to end. (8:**9**:10:**12** sts)

Size 6–12 months, fasten off.

Row 15: 1tr in each st to last 2 sts, tr2tog. (8:**9**:10:**11** sts)

Size 12–18 months, fasten off.

Sleeves (make 2)

Using A, make 27:**33**:37:**37**ch.

Row 1: 1ch, 1dc in each ch to end. (26:**32**:36:**36** sts)

Row 2: 1ch, 1dc in each st to end. (26:**32**:36:**36** sts)

Row 3: 3ch, 1tr in each st to end.

Row 4: 3ch, 2tr in next st, 1tr in each st to last 2 sts, 2tr in next st, 1tr in top of 3-ch from previous row. (29:**35**:39:**39** sts)

Rows 5–6: 3ch, 1tr in each st to last st, 1tr in top of 3-ch from previous row. (30:**36**:40:**40** sts)

Row 7: 3ch, 1tr in next st, 2tr in next st, 1tr in each st to last 2 sts, 2tr in next st, 1tr in next st, 1tr in top of 3-ch from previous row. (33:**39**:43:**43** sts)

Row 8: 3ch, 1tr in each st to end, 1tr in top of 3-ch from previous row. (34:**40**:44:**44** sts)

Row 9: 3ch, 1tr in each st to end, 1tr in top of 3-ch from previous row. (35:**41**:45:**45** sts)

Size 0–3 months only:

Row 10: Rep Row 8. (36 sts)

Work straight in tr until sleeve measures 12.5cm (5in).

All other sizes:
Row 10: Rep Row 7. (**44**:**48**:**48** sts)
Row 11: Rep Row 8. (**45**:**49**:**49** sts)
Row 12: Rep Row 8. (**46**:**50**:**50** sts)
Row 13: Rep Row 8. (**47**:**51**:**51** sts)
   Rep Row 7 [0:0:1] times more. (**47**:**51**:**54** sts)
Work straight in tr until sleeve measures 12.5:**15.5**:19.5:**24**cm (5:**6¼**:7¾:**9½**in).

All sizes shape top:
Next row: Ss across first 2:**3**:3:**4** sts, tr2tog, 1tr in each st to last 4:**5**:5:**6** sts, tr2tog, turn. (30:**39**:43:**44** sts)
Next row: [Tr2tog] twice, 1tr in each st to last 4 sts, [tr2tog] twice. (26:**35**:39:**40** sts)
   Rep the last row 3:**4**:5:**5** more times. (14:**19**:19:**20** sts)
   Fasten off.

Finishing
Pin and oversew shoulder seams together. With right sides together, oversew sleeves from underarm to wrist.

   Fit each sleeve inside main piece with wrong sides on the inside. Match centre top of sleeve to match to shoulder seam and sleeve seam to match missed 3 sts of main body.

   Pin and oversew.

Edging
Fronts, back and bottom:
Using A, join yarn bottom right-hand front edge with RS facing.

   Make 1dc evenly around right side, across back neck, down left side to bottom corner and along bottom edge, join with a ss in first dc.

   Fasten off.

Picot edging:
Using B, join yarn in first dc at base of front right-hand edge with RS facing.

   *3ch, ss in same st, miss 1 st, ss in next st;

rep from * around cardigan edging. Ss in base of first picot to finish.

   Fasten off.

Sleeve edging:
Using B, join yarn at the seam, make a Picot edging around as main body.

Ties
Using B, join yarn at Row 3 of right front edge. Make 102:**120**:134:**148**ch, 1dc in next ch from

hook and each ch back to front edge, join with ss. Fasten off leaving a long tail. Sew in end securely.

   Rep Tie instructions on other front edge.

Finishing
Sew in ends.

   Tie ties to fit by slotting one tie through treble holes when fitted on baby.

Simple Stripy Tank Top

Striped in bright colours, this works well over trousers or a skirt and keeps your baby nice and snug.

Back

Each row is alternated between A and B to form one-row stripes.

Using A, make 46:**50**:54:**58**ch.

Row 1 (RS): 1htr in third ch from hook, 1htr in each ch to end. (44:**48**:52:**56** sts)

Next row (WS): Using B, 2ch, 1htr in each st.

Cont working straight, striping rows, until work measures 16.5:**16.5**:20:**23**cm (6½:**6½**:8:**9¼**in) ending with a RS row.

Fasten off.

Armholes:

Row 1 (WS facing): Miss 5 sts, rejoin yarn in next st, 2ch, 1htr in each of next 34:**38**:42:**46** sts, leaving last 5 sts unworked. (34:**38**:42:**46** sts) **

Cont working straight until armhole measures 11.5:**11.5**:13:**13**cm (4½:**4½**:5¼:**5¼**in).

Shoulders:

Next row: 2ch, work 11:**12**:13:**14** sts.

Fasten off.

Miss next 12:**14**:16:**18** sts, rejoin yarn in next st, 2ch, 1htr in each of rem 11:**12**:13:**14** sts.

Fasten off.

Front

Work to ** as for back.

Next two rows: 2ch, 1htr in each st to end. Divide for neck.

Neck side 1:

Row 1 (WS): 2ch, 1htr in each of next 17:**19**:21:**23** sts. (17:**19**:21:**23** sts)

Row 2: 2ch, miss 1 st (neck edge), 1htr in each st to end. (16:**18**:20:**22** sts)

Row 3: 2ch, 1htr in each st to last 2 sts, htr2tog (neck edge). (15:**17**:19:**21** sts)

Rep Rows 2 and 3 until 11:**12**:13:**14** sts rem.

Work 2ch, 1htr in each st to end until front measures same length as back.

Neck side 2:

With WS facing, work Side 2 to match Side 1 reversing shaping.

Fasten off.

Finishing

Join shoulder and side seams.

Lower edging:

Using C and with RS facing, join yarn to lower edge at one of the side seams, 1ch, work a round of dc evenly along lower edge, ss in first ch to join round.

Fasten off.

Neck edging:

Using C and with RS facing, join yarn at neck edge of one of the shoulder seams.

1ch, make 1dc evenly around neck edge, join with a ss in first ch.

Fasten off.

Armhole edging:

Using C and with RS facing, join yarn to top of one of the side seams, 1ch, work a round of dc evenly around armhole, join with a ss in first ch.

Fasten off.

Rep for second armhole.

Sew in ends.

Materials

Rooster Almerino DK

→ 1:**1**:2:**2** x 50g (1¾oz) balls – approx 112.5:**112.5**:225:**225**m (124:**124**:248:**248**yds) – each of shade 201 Cornish (off white) (A) and shade 210 Custard (yellow) (B)

→ 1 x 50g (1¾oz) ball – approx 112.5m (124yds) – of shade 217 Beach (turquoise blue) (C)

→ 4mm (F/5) crochet hook

Abbreviations

ch chain; **cont** continue; **dc** double crochet; **htr** half treble; **rem** remaining; **RS** right side; **ss** slip stitch; **st(s)** stitches; **WS** wrong side; **yrh** yarn round hook

Special abbreviation

htr2tog (half treble 2 together decrease) *yrh, insert hook in next st, yrh, pull yarn through (3 loops on hook). Without finishing st, rep from * in next st (5 loops on hook), yrh, pull yarn through all 5 loops on hook

Size

To fit age: 3–6:**6–12**:12–18:**24–36** months

Finished size

Chest	(cm):	52.5	**56.5**	62.5	**65**
	(in):	21	**22½**	25	**26**
Length	(cm):	27.5	**27.5**	32.5	**36.5**
	(in):	11	**11**	13	**14½**
Armhole to shoulder	(cm):	12	**12**	14	**14**
	(in):	4¾	**4¾**	5½	**5½**

Tension

17 sts x 13 rows over a 10cm (4in) square working half treble using a 4mm (F/5) hook.

Baby Shell Cardigan

A really pretty cardigan for a new baby in the family.
It was inspired by an old vintage-style pattern,
but making it using modern wools and adding flower
embellishments gives it a modern, yet retro twist.

Materials

Rooster Almerino Baby

→ 4:**4** x 50g (1¾oz) balls – approx 500:**500**m (546:**546**yds) – of shade 511 Anenome (purple) (A)

→ Small amounts of three different shades of pink (B)

→ 3mm (D/3) and 2.5mm (C/2) crochet hooks

→ 3 buttons

Abbreviations

ch chain; **cont** continue; **dc** double crochet; **htr** half treble; **inc** increase; **rep** repeat; **ss** slip stitch; **st(s)** stitches; **tr** treble; **WS** wrong side

Size

To fit age: 0–3:**3–6** months

Finished size

Chest	(cm):	47.5	55
	(in):	19	22
Length	(cm):	22.5	27.5
	(in):	9	11
Sleeve seam	(cm):	10	10
	(in):	4	4

Tension

4 groups of shell pattern x 6 rows of shell pattern over a 10cm (4in) square using 3mm (D/3) hook.

Yoke

Starting at neck edge, and using 3mm (D/3) hook and A, make 60:**71**ch.

Row 1: 1tr in third ch from hook, 1tr in each ch. (58:**69** sts)

Row 2: 3ch, miss first st, 1tr in each st to end, 1tr in third of 3-ch from previous row.

Row 3: 3ch, miss first st, 1tr in each of next 2:**3** sts, *2tr in next st (inc made), 1tr in each of next 4:**5** tr; rep from * 9 times more, 2tr in next st (inc made), 1tr in each of next 3 sts, 1tr in third of 3-ch from previous row. (69:**80** sts)

Row 4: Rep Row 2.

Row 5: 3ch, miss first st, 1tr in each of next 3:**4** sts, *inc in next st, 1tr in each of next 5:**6** sts, rep from * 9 times more, inc in next st, 1tr in each of next 3 sts, 1tr in third of 3-ch. (80:**91** sts)

Row 6: 3ch, miss first st, 1tr in each st, working inc above inc on previous row, ending with 1tr in third of 3-ch. (91:**102** sts)

Rep Row 6 three times more. (124:**135** sts)

Row 10: 3ch, miss first st, 1tr in each of next 4:**5** sts, inc in next st, 1tr in each of next 33:**35** sts, inc in next st, * 1tr in each of next 10:**11** sts, inc in next st; rep from * 3 times more, 1tr in each of next 33:**35** sts, inc in next st, 1tr in each of next 5:**7** sts, 1tr in third of 3-ch. (131:**142** sts)

Row 11: 3ch, miss first st, 1tr in each of next 5:**7** sts, inc in next st, 1tr in each of next 12:**14** sts, make 8:**10**ch, miss next 28:**28** sts, 1tr in each of next 6:**7** sts, inc in next st, 1tr in each

of next 23:**25** sts, inc in next st, 1tr in each of next 6:**7** sts, make 8:**10**ch, miss next 25:**27** sts, 1tr in each of next 12:**14** sts, inc in next st, 1tr in each of next 5:**6** sts, 1tr in third of 3-ch. (79:**90** sts)

Row 12: 2ch, miss first st, 1dc in each of next 19:**23** sts, 1dc into each of next 8:**10**ch, 1dc into each of next 39:**43** sts, 1dc into each of next 8:**10**ch, 1dc into each of next 19:**22** sts, 1dc in third of 3-ch. (95:**110** sts)

Do not fasten off.

Skirt 0–3 months:

Row 1: 1dc in first dc, *miss 1dc, 5tr in next dc (shell made), miss 1dc, 1dc in next dc, miss 2dc, shell in next dc, miss 2dc, 1dc in

next dc; rep from * 8 times more, miss 1dc, 5tr in next dc, miss 1dc, 1dc in next dc.

Skirt 3–6 months:

Row 1: 1dc in first dc, *miss 1dc, 5tr in next dc (shell made), miss 1dc, 1dc in next dc, miss 2dc, shell in next dc, miss 2dc, 1dc in next dc; rep from * 9 times more, miss 1dc, 5tr in next dc, miss 1dc, 1dc in next dc, miss 2dc, shell in next dc, miss 1dc, 1dc in next dc.

Both sizes:

Row 2: 3ch, 2tr in first st (half shell made), *1dc in centre tr of next shell, shell in next dc; rep from * ending with 1dc in centre tr of last shell, 3tr in last dc.

Row 3: 1ch, 1dc in first tr, *shell in next dc, 1dc in centre tr of shell; rep from * ending with shell in last dc, 1dc in 3-ch. 3ch.

Rep last 2 rows until skirt measures 12.5:**17.5**cm (5:**7**in) or length required, ending with a 3rd pattern row.

Fasten off.

Sleeves

Round 1: Attach yarn to 4th:**5th** of 8:**10**ch at underarm, 1dc in each ch, 1dc in each of next 2 row ends, 1dc in next 28:**28** sts, 1dc in each of next 2 row ends, 1dc in each ch, 1ss in first dc. (36:**38** sts)

Round 2: *Miss 2 dc, shell in next dc, miss 2 dc, 1dc in next dc; rep from * 6 times more, working last dc in ss.

Round 3: 1ss in each of first 2tr, 1dc in next tr, *shell in next dc, 1dc in centre tr of next shell;

sleeves 6in. 3.00 hooks then 2 56h

sleeves.
one Row triple dc
then double crochet

rep from * 6 times more, omitting 1dc at end
of last rep, 1ss in first dc.

Rep Round 3 row until sleeve measures
10:**12.5**cm (4:**5**in).

Fasten off.

Edging

With RS facing, and using 3mm (D/3) hook
and A, attach yarn to neck edge of left front,
1dc in same place as join, *shell in next row
end, 1dc in next row end; rep from * 4 times
more, shell in next dc row end, 1dc in next dc
row end. Cont in this manner down front
edges making 1 shell in lower edge corner of
each front, 1ss in first dc.

Fasten off.

Flowers (make 6 in different shades of pink)

Using 2.5mm (C/2) hook and B, make 4ch,
join with a ss to form a ring.

*2ch, 1htr in ring, 2ch, ss in ring; rep from *
4 times more (5 petals).

Fasten off.

Sew in ends, weaving around centre to
close hole in ring.

Thread yarn needle with contrast colour
and embroider a French knot in the centre.

Finishing

Sew in ends. Sew 3 buttons to edge of yoke to
match position of buttonholes in overlap.
Sew flowers at base of yoke.

6 in

Pocket Trim Cardigan

A really simple cardigan to make, with a pretty 'granny square' pocket trim.

Materials

Rooster Almerino DK

→ 3:**3**:4:**4**:5:**5** x 50g (1¾oz) balls – approx 337.5:**337.5**:450:**450**:562.5:**562.5**m (372:**372**:496:**496**:620:**620**yds) – of shade 205 Glace (light blue) (A)

→ 1 x 50g (1¾oz) ball – approx 112.5m (124yds) – each of shade 219 Sandcastle (pale yellow) (B) and 201 Cornish (off white) (C)

→ 4:**4**:4:**4**:4:**5** buttons

→ 4mm (F/5) and 3.5mm (E/4) crochet hooks

Abbreviations

ch chain; **dc** double crochet; **dc2tog** (double crochet 2 together decrease) insert hook in next st, yrh, pull yarn through (2 loops on hook). Without finishing st, insert hook in next st, yrh, pull yarn through (3 loops on hook), yrh, pull yarn through all 3 loops on hook; **htr** half treble; **rep** repeat; **RS** right side; **ss** slip stitch; **st(s)** stitch(es); **tr** treble; **yrh** yarn round hook

Special abbreviations

tr2tog (treble 2 together decrease) yrh, insert hook in next st, yrh, pull yarn through, yrh, pull yarn through 2 loops on hook (2 loops), yrh, insert hook in next st, yrh, pull yarn through, yrh, pull yarn through 2 loops on hook (3 loops), yrh, pull yarn through all 3 loops on hook

tr3tog (treble 3 together decrease) yrh, insert hook in next st, yrh, pull yarn through, yrh, pull yarn through 2 loops on hook (2 loops), yrh, insert hook in next st, yrh, pull yarn through, yrh, pull yarn through 2 loops on hook (3 loops), yrh, insert hook in next st, yrh, pull yarn through, yrh, pull yarn through 2 loops on hook (4 loops), yrh, pull yarn through all 4 loops on hook

Size

To fit age: 0–3:**3–6**:6–12:**12–18**:18–24:**24–36** months

Finished size

Chest	(cm)	47.5	**51.5**	62.5	**65**	67.5	70
	(in)	19	**20½**	25	**26**	27	28
Length	(cm)	26.5	**26.5**	29	**32.5**	35	37.5
	(in)	10½	**10½**	11½	**13**	14	15
Sleeve seam	(cm)	10	**10**	11.5	**12.5**	14	14.5
	(in)	4	**4**	4½	**5**	5½	5¾

Tension

18 sts x 10 rows over a 10cm (4in) square working half treble using a 3mm (D/3) hook.

Back

Using A and 4mm ((F/5) hook, make 33:**37**:41:**45**:49:**53**ch.

Row 1: 1htr in third ch from hook and in each ch to end. (31:**35**:39:**43**:47:**49** sts)

Row 2: 2ch, 1htr in each st to end.

Rep Row 2 until work measures 15:**15**:17.5:**20**:21.5:**22.5**cm (6:**6**:7:**8**:8½:**9**in).

Do not fasten off.

Add sleeves to back:

Make 16:**20**:24:**28**:32:**36**ch, turn.

Row 1: 1htr in third ch from hook, 1htr in each st across back to end of row, make 16:**20**:24:**28**:32:**36**ch for second sleeve, turn.

Row 2: 1htr in third ch from hook, 1htr in each st to end of row.

Row 3: 2ch, 1htr in each st to end.

Rep Row 3 until a total of 12:**12**:14:**15**:17:**18** rows have been completed on right sleeve, 11:**11**:13:**14**:16:**17** rows on left sleeve.

Fasten off.

Front (make left and right fronts the same)

Using A and 4mm ((F/5) hook, make 17:**19**:21:**23**:25:**27**ch, turn.

Row 1: 1htr in third ch from hook and in each ch to end. (15:**17**:19:**21**:23:**25** sts)

Row 2: 2ch, 1htr in next and each st to end. Rep Row 2 and work as for back to underarm.

Add sleeves to front:

Make 16:**20**:24:**28**:32:**36**ch, turn.

Next row: 1htr in third ch from hook, 1htr in each st across front to end. (29:**35**:41:**47**:53:**59** sts)

Next row: 2ch, 1htr in each st to end.

Rep last row until 8:**8**:8:**10**:10:**12** rows have been completed ending at sleeve edge.

Neck shaping:

Next row: 2ch, 1htr across 23:**29**:34:**38**:43:**46** sts, leaving 6:**6**:7:**9**:10:**13** sts unworked.

Next row: 2ch, 1htr in each st to sleeve edge. Rep last row twice more.

Fasten off.

When working on second front, start with RS facing and make sleeve ch at opposite end to first front.

With RS together, join shoulder seams with ss, working in back loops only.

Sleeve cuffs:

With RS facing, join yarn in first st, make 1ch, turn.

Row 1: 1dc in each row end along edge of sleeve. (23:**23**:27:**29**:33:**35** sts)

Row 2: 1ch, 1dc in next 2 sts, [dc2tog, 1dc in each of next 2:**2**:3:**3**:4:**4** sts] 5 times, 1dc in each st to end. (18:**18**:22:**24**:28:**30** sts)

Row 3: 1ch, 1dc in first and each st to end. Rep last row 3 times more.

Fasten off.

With RS together, join side seams and sleeve seams.

Buttonbands

Left side:

With RS facing, join yarn in top neck edge.

Row 1: 1ch, make 34:**34**:37:**40**:42:**44** sts along front edge.

Row 2: 1ch, 1dc in each st to end.

Row 3 (buttonhole row): 1ch, 1dc in first st, *2ch, miss 2 sts, 1dc in each of next 5:**5**:6:**7**:7:**7** sts; rep from * 3 times more, 1dc in each st to end of row.

Row 4: 1ch, 1dc in each st to end, making 2dc in each buttonhole space.

Row 5: 1ch, 1dc in each st to end. Fasten off.

Right side:

With RS facing, join yarn at bottom front edge.

Row 1: 1ch, make 34:**34**:37:**40**:42:**44** sts along front edge.

Row 2: 1ch, 1dc in each st to end. Rep Row 2 three times more.

Fasten off.

Neck edging

With RS facing, join yarn with ss at right front edge.

1ch, 4dc across front band, 17:**17**:19:**21**:24:**27** sts across right front neck, 1dc in each st across back, 17:**17**:19:**21**:24:**27** sts across left neck, 4dc across front band.

Next row: 1ch, 1dc in each st around neck edge.

Rep last row once more.

Fasten off.

Pocket

Using B and 3.5mm (E/4) hook, make 6ch, ss in first ch to form a ring.

Round 1: 3ch, tr2tog in ring *3ch, tr3tog in ring, 2ch, tr3tog in ring; rep from * twice more, 3ch, tr3tog in ring, 2ch ss in top of first 3-ch. Fasten off B.

Round 2: Join in C to any 3-ch sp, 3ch, tr2tog in same 3-ch sp, *3ch, tr3tog in same sp, 1ch, 3tr in next 2ch sp, 1ch, tr3tog in next 3-ch sp; rep from * twice more, 3ch, tr3tog in same sp, 1ch, 3tr in next 2-ch sp, 1ch, ss in top of first 3-ch. Fasten off C.

Round 3: Join in A into fasten off st, 1dc in top of first tr3tog from previous round, *3dc in corner ch sp, 1dc in top of next tr3tog from previous round, 1dc in next ch sp, 1dc in top of each of next 3 tr, 1dc in next ch sp, 1dc in top of next tr3tog from previous round; rep from * twice more. 3dc in corner ch sp, 1dc in top of next tr3tog from previous round, 1dc in next ch sp, 1dc in top of each of next 3 tr, 1dc in next ch sp, ss in first dc.

Fasten off.

Finishing

Attach pocket to bottom of left front edge by sewing sides and bottom, leaving the top open for the pocket opening.

Sew in ends.

Flower Power Cardigan

A very easy and sweet little cardigan, to suit even a newborn, this is a simple project that is suitable for beginners.

Materials

Rooster Almerino Baby

→ 1:2:3:3:4:5 x 50g (1¾oz) balls – approx 125:**250**:375:**375**:500:**625**m (136.5:**273**:409.5:**409.5**:546:**682.5**yds) – of shade 504 Seaweed (pale green) (MC)

→ Scraps of lilac, white, dark pink, light pink, mid pink

→ 3mm (D/3) crochet hook

→ 3–6 buttons (depending on size)

Abbreviations

ch chain; **dc** double crochet; **dc2tog** (double crochet 2 together decrease) insert hook in next st, yrh, pull yarn through (2 loops on hook). Without finishing st, insert hook in next st, yrh, pull yarn through (3 loops on hook), yrh, pull yarn through all 3 loops on hook; **MC** main colour; **rep** repeat; **ss** slip stitch; **st(s)** stitch(es); **tr** treble; **yrh** yarn round hook

Size

To fit age: Newborn:**0–3**:3–6:**6–12**:12–24:**24–36**

Finished

Chest:	(cm):	30	37.5	47.5	57.5	67.5	77.5
	(in):	12	15	19	23	27	31
Length:	(cm):	17.5	21.5	25	29	32.5	36.5
	(in):	7	8½	10	11½	13	14½
Sleeve seam	(cm):	11.5	12.5	16.5	20	25	27.5
	(in):	4½	5	6½	8	10	11

Tension

15 sts x 9 rows over a 10cm (4in) square working treble using a 3mm (D/3) hook.

Back and sides

Made in one piece starting at neck edge and working down from top.

Using MC, make 36:**48**:60:**72**:84:**96**ch.

Row 1: 1tr in fourth ch from hook, 1tr in each of next 3:**5**:7:**9**:11:**13** ch, 3tr in next ch, 1tr in each of next 5:**7**:9:**11**:13:**15** ch, 3tr in next ch, 1tr in each of next 10:**14**:18:**22**:26:**30** ch, 3tr in next ch, 1tr in each of next 5:**7**:9:**11**:13:**15** ch, 3tr in next ch, 1tr in each of last 5:**7**:9:**11**:13:**15** ch.

Rows 2–5: 3ch, 1tr in each st, 3tr in top of middle st of each of 3-tr group of previous row.

Row 6: 3ch, 1tr in each st to middle of first 3-tr group. 1tr in top of 3-tr group, 4:**5**:6:**7**:8:**9**ch, miss each st of previous row to next 3-tr group, 1tr in top of middle st of 3-tr group and in each st across to middle of third 3-tr group, 4:**5**:6:**7**:8:**9**ch, miss each st of previous row to next 3-tr group, 1tr in top of middle st of 3-tr group and in each st to end.

Row 7: 3ch, 1tr in each st and 1tr in each ch along row to end.

Rows 8–15:**19**:23:**27**:31:**35**: 3ch, 1tr in each st to end, 2ch at end of last row.

Edging

Left front edge:

Turn to work up left front edge.

Row 1: Work 25:**30**:35:**40**:45:**50**dc evenly up side of left front, 1ch, turn.

Row 2: 1dc in each st back down front, 1ch, turn.

Row 3: 1dc in each st, 1ch, turn.

Row 4: 1dc in each st to last st, 3dc in last st.

Bottom edge:

Work 1dc evenly along bottom edge, 3dc in last st.

Right front edge:

Row 1: Work 25:**30**:35:**40**:45:**50**dc evenly up side of right front, 1ch, turn

Row 2: 1dc in each st, 1ch, turn.

Place markers down right front edge at buttonhole positions.

Buttonholes:

Row 3: For each buttonhole: 1dc in each st to marker point, *miss 2 sts, 2ch, 1dc in each st to next marker point; rep from * to last buttonhole, 1dc in each st to end.

Row 4: 1ch, 1dc in each st to end, making 2dc in buttonhole ch sps, 3dc in last st.

Fasten off.

Neck edge:

Join yarn at top edge of right hand front, 1dc evenly around neck edge, making dc2tog after every fifth st to bring neck edge in.

Fasten off.

Sleeves

Join yarn in centre st at bottom of armhole.

Round 1: 3ch, 1tr in each st around armhole, join with a ss in top of first 3-ch.

Rounds 2–8:9:12:16:22:24: 3ch, 1tr in each tr, ss in top of first 3-ch.

Round 9:10:13:17:23:25: 1ch, 1dc in each st to end, ss in top of first ch.

Fasten off.

Flowers

Using different colour for each flower, make 4ch, ss in first ch to make a ring.

*3ch, 2tr in ring, 3ch, ss in ring; rep from * until 5 petals are made.

Fasten off leaving a long end.

Using long end in yarn needle weave around centre to close circle.

Using contrast colour, make French knot in centre of each flower, wrapping wool around needle five times.

Finishing

Sew on buttons. Sew flowers around neck and bottom edge.

Ship Ahoy Jumper

A bright and cheery striped jumper with an embroidered anchor. A very simple design made using half trebles.

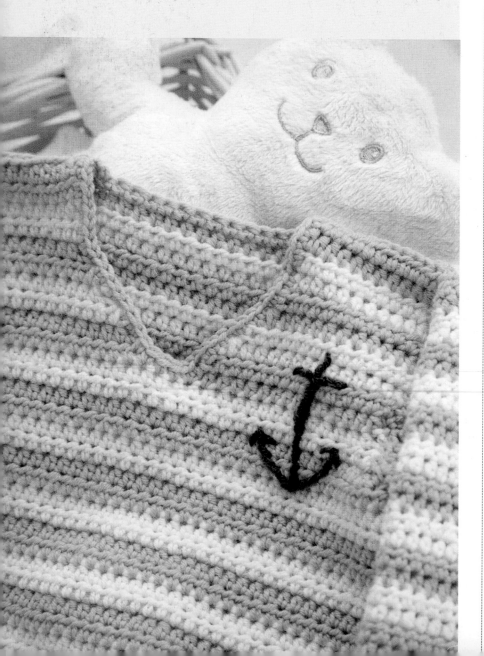

Materials

Rooster Almerino Baby

→ 2:2:2:3 x 50g (1¾oz) balls – approx 250:**250**:250:**375**m (273:**273**:273:**409.5**yds) – each of shade 510 Mermaid (aqua blue) (A) and 501 Sea Spray (white) (B)

→ Scrap of dark blue

→ 3mm (D/3) crochet hook

Abbreviations

ch chain; **cont** continue; **dc** double crochet; **rem** remaining; **rep** repeat; **RS** right side; **ss** slip stitch; **st(s)** stitch(es); **WS** wrong side; **yrh** yarn round hook

Special abbreviation

htr2tog (half treble 2 together decrease) *yrh, insert hook in next st, yrh, pull yarn through (3 loops on hook). Without finishing st, rep from * in next st (5 loops on hook), yrh, pull yarn through all 5 loops on hook

Size

To fit age: 3–6:**6–12**:12–18:**24–36** months

Finished size

Chest	**(cm)**:	51.5	56.5	61.5	64
	(in):	20½	22½	24½	25½
Length	**(cm)**:	30	30	34	39
	(in):	12	12	13½	15½
Sleeve seam	**(cm)**:	11.5	11.5	11.5	14.5
	(in):	4½	4½	4½	5¾

Tension

18 sts x 15 rows over a 10cm (4in) square working half treble using a 3mm (D/3) hook.

Back

Alternate colours every second row throughout.

Using A, make 46:**50**:54:**58**ch.

Row 1 (RS): 1htr in third ch from hook, 1htr in each ch to end. (44:**48**:52:**56** sts)

Row 2: 2ch, 1htr in each st.

Join in B.

*Using B, rep Row 2 twice.

Using A, rep Row 2 twice.

Rep from * until work measures 19:**19**:21.5:**24**cm (7½:**7½**:8½:**9½**in) ending with a RS row.

Fasten off.

Armholes:

Row 1 (WS): Miss each of next 5 sts, join yarn into next st, 2ch, 1htr into each of next 34:**38**:42:**46** sts, leaving last 5 sts unworked, turn. (34:**38**:42:**46** sts)**

Cont working straight until armhole measures 11.5:**11.5**:11.5:**13**cm (4½:**4½**:4½:**5¼**in).

Shoulders:

Next row: 2ch, work 11:**12**:13:**14** sts.

Fasten off.

Miss next 12:**14**:16:**18** sts, rejoin yarn into next st, 2ch, 1htr into each of rem 11:**12**:13:**14** sts.

Fasten off.

Front

Work as for back until **.

Next two rows: 2ch, 1htr into each st to end.

Neck side 1:

Row 1 (WS): 2ch, 1htr in each of next 17:**19**:21:**23** sts. (17:**19**:21:**23** sts)

Row 2: 2ch, miss 1 st (neck edge), 1htr in each st to end. (16:**18**:20:**22** sts)

Row 3: 2ch, 1htr in each st to last 2 sts, htr2tog (neck edge). (15:**17**:19:**21** sts)

Rep Rows 2 and 3 until 12:**13**:13:**14** sts rem.

Work 2ch, 1htr in each st to end until front measures same length as back.

Neck side 2:

With WS facing, work side 2 to match side 1, reversing shaping.

Sew in all loose ends.

Sleeves

Make 28:**28**:30:**32**ch.

1htr in third ch from hook, 1htr in each ch to end. (26:**26**:28:**30** sts)

Rows 1–2: 2ch, 1htr in each st to end.

Row 3: 2ch, 2htr into first st, 1htr to last st, 2htr in last st. (28:**28**:30:**32** sts)

Row 4: Rep Row 3. (30:**30**:32:**34** sts)

Row 5: Rep Row 3. (32:**32**:34:**36** sts)

Rep last 4 rows until there are 42:**42**:42:**46** sts.

Cont to work in htr without increasing until work measures 17.5:**20**:22.5:**27.5**cm (7:**8**:9:**11**in).

Fasten off.

Finishing

Block pieces and steam gently.

Join shoulder seams.

With WS facing, place a pin marker at centre of the top of sleeve. Pin sleeve at pin marker to shoulder seam and pin sleeve around armhole edge. Sew in place.

Lower edging:

With RS facing and using B, join yarn to lower edge at one of side seams, 1ch, work a round of dc evenly along lower edge. Ss into first ch to join round.

Fasten off, sew in ends.

Neck edging:

With RS facing join yarn at neck edge of one of shoulder seams, 1ch, make 1dc evenly around neck edge, join with ss into first ch.

Fasten off.

Using scrap of dark blue, embroider an anchor onto top left-hand shoulder.

Heart Tank Top

This is a really useful top; it's easy to slip on over a T-shirt and very comfortable to wear. When crocheting intarsia, use separate balls of wool for each side and join in the new colour on the stitch before.

Materials

Rooster Almerino DK

→ 2:**2**:3:**3** x 50g (1¾oz) balls – approx 225:**225**:337.5:**337.5**m (248:**248**:372:**372**yds) – of shade 203 Strawberry Cream (light pink) (A)

→ 1 x 50g (1¾oz) ball – approx 112.5m (124yds) – of shade 201 Cornish (cream) (B)

→ 4mm (F/5) crochet hook

Abbreviations

ch chain; **cont** continue; **dc** double crochet; **foll** following; **htr** half treble; **rem** remaining; **rep** repeat; **RS** right side; **ss** slip stitch; **st(s)** stitches; **WS** wrong side; **yrh** yarn round hook

Special abbreviation

htr2tog (half treble 2 together decrease) *yrh, insert hook in next st, yrh, pull yarn through (3 loops on hook). Without finishing st, rep from * in next st (5 loops on hook), yrh, pull yarn through all 5 loops on hook

Size

To fit age: 3–6:**6–12**:12–18:**24–36** months

Finished size

Chest	(cm):	52.5	**56.5**	62.5	65
	(in):	21	**22½**	25	26
Length	(cm):	29	**31.5**	32.5	36.5
	(in):	11½	**12½**	13	14½
Armhole to shoulder	(cm):	10	**11.5**	11.5	12.5
	(in):	4	**4½**	4½	5

Tension

17 sts x 13 rows over a 10cm (4in) square working half treble using a 4mm (F/5) hook.

Back

Using A, make 47:**51**:55:**59**ch.

Row 1 (RS): 1htr in third ch from hook, 1htr in next and each ch to end. (45:**49**:53:**57** sts)

Next row: 2ch, 1htr in each st.

Cont working straight until work is 24:**28**:28:**30** rows ending with a WS row.

Fasten off.

Armholes:

Row 1 (RS facing): Miss 5 sts, join yarn in next st, 2ch, 1htr in each of next 35:**39**:43:**47** sts, leaving last 5 sts unworked. (35:**39**:43:**47** sts)

Cont working straight until armhole measures 10:**11.5**:11.5:**12.5**cm (4:**4½**:4½:**5**in).

Shoulders:

Next row: 2ch, work 11:**12**:12:**13** sts.

Fasten off.

Miss next 13:**15**:15:**19** sts, rejoin yarn in next st, 2ch, 1htr in each of rem 11:**12**:12:**13** sts.

Fasten off.

Front

Using A, make 47:**51**:55:**59**ch.

Work first 3:**7**:7:**9** rows as back. (45:**49**:53:**57** sts)

Heart motif:

With WS facing, start with Row 1 of chart using Intarsia method and B for heart motif. First heart motif st is the 23rd:**25th**:25th:**27th**. Work with 2 separate balls of A when working from chart plus third ball for top indent in heart.

Next row: Using A, 2ch, 1htr in each st to end.

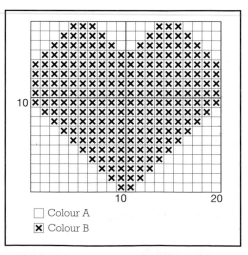

☐ Colour A
☒ Colour B

Fasten off.

Armholes:

Row 1 (RS facing): Miss first 5 sts, rejoin yarn in next st, 2ch, 1htr in each of next 35:**39**:43:**47** sts, leaving last 5 sts unworked, turn. (35:**39**:43:**47** sts)

Rows 2–3: 2ch, 1htr in each st to end.

Divide for neck.

Neck Side 1 (right neck edging):

Row 1 (WS facing): 2ch, 1htr in each of foll 17:**19**:21:**23** sts, turn.

Row 2: 2ch, miss 1 st (neck edge), 1htr in each st to end.

Row 3: 2ch, 1htr in each st to last 2 sts, htr2tog (neck edge). (15:**17**:19:**21** sts)

Rep Rows 2 and 3 until 11:**12**:12:**13** sts rem.

Work 2ch, 1htr in each st to end until front measures same length as back.

Fasten off.

Neck Side 2:

With WS facing, miss 1 st at beginning of neck edge, rejoin yarn in next st.

Row 1 (WS facing): 2ch, 1htr in each of foll 17:**19**:21:**23** sts.

Work Side 2 to match Side 1, reversing shaping.

Finishing

Block pieces and steam gently. Join shoulder and side seams. Sew in ends.

Lower edging:

Using B and with RS facing, join yarn to lower edge at one of the side seams, 1ch, work a round of dc evenly along lower edge, ss in first ch to join round.

Fasten off.

Neck edging:

With RS facing join yarn at neck edge of one of the shoulder seams.

1ch, make 1dc evenly around neck edge, join with a ss in first ch.

Fasten off.

Armhole edging:

With RS facing join yarn to top of one of the side seams, 1ch, work a round of dc evenly around armhole, join with a ss in first ch.

Fasten off.

Rep for second armhole.

Pompom Cardigan

This is a really popular cardigan; pretty pompoms and a frill edge make it a cute baby garment. Don't make the pompoms too thick – loose and fluffy ones are much kinder on the neck.

Materials

Rooster Almerino DK

→ 3:**3**:4:**4**:5:**5** x 50g (1¾oz) balls – approx 337.5:**337.5**:450:**450**:562.5:**562.5**m (372:**372**:496:**496**:620:**620**yds) – of shade 220 Lighthouse (red) (A)

→ Scraps of shade 201 Seashell (off white) (B), 205 Glace (light blue) (C), 218 Starfish (orange) (D), 216 Pier (green) (E), 208 Ocean (blue) (F)

→ 3.5mm (E/4) crochet hook size

→ 3 buttons

Abbreviations

ch chain; **dc** double crochet; **dc2tog** (double crochet 2 together decrease) insert hook in next st, yrh, pull yarn through (2 loops on hook). Without finishing st, insert hook in next st, yrh, pull yarn through (3 loops on hook), yrh, pull yarn through all 3 loops on hook; **htr** half treble; **rep** repeat; **RS** right side; **ss** slip stitch; **st(s)** stitch(es); **tr** treble; **yrh** yarn round hook

Special abbreviation

Shell 1dc, miss 2 sts, 5tr in next st, miss 2 sts (1 shell made)

Size

To fit age: 0–3:**3–6**:6–12:**12–18**:18–24:**24–36** months

Finished size

Chest	(cm):	47.5	**51.5**	62.5	**65**	67.5	**70**
	(in):	19	**20½**	25	**26**	27	**28**
Length	(cm):	26.5	**26.5**	29	**32.5**	35	**37.5**
	(in):	10½	**10½**	11½	**13**	14	**15**
Sleeve seam	(cm):	10	**10**	11.5	**12.5**	14	**14.5**
	(in):	4	**4**	4½	**5**	5½	**5¾**

Tension

16 sts x 10 rows over a 10cm (4in) square working half treble using a 3.5mm (E/4) hook.

Back

Using A, make 33:**37**:41:**45**:49:**53**ch.

Row 1: 1htr in third ch from hook and each ch to end. (31:**35**:39:**43**:47:**49** sts)

Row 2: 2ch, 1htr in each st to end.

Rep Row 2 until 20:**20**:24:**26**:26:**28** rows have been worked.

Do not fasten off.

Add sleeves:

Make 16:**20**:24:**28**:32:**36**ch, turn.

Row 1: 1htr in third ch from hook, 1htr in each st across the back to end of row, make 16:**20**:24:**28**:32:**36**ch for second sleeve, turn.

Row 2: 1htr in third ch from hook, 1htr in each st to end of row.

Row 3: 2ch, 1htr in each st to end.

Rep Row 3 until a total of 12:**12**:14:**15**:17:**18** rows have been completed on right sleeve, 11:**11**:13:**14**:16:**17** rows on left sleeve.

Fasten off.

Front (make left and right fronts the same)

Make 17:**19**:21:**23**:25:**27**ch, turn.

Row 1: 1htr in third ch from hook and in each ch to end. (15:**17**:19:**21**:23:**25** sts)

Row 2: 2ch, 1htr in each st to end.

Rep Row 2 and work as for back to underarm.

Add sleeves:

Make 16:**20**:24:**28**:32:**36**ch, turn.

Next row: 1htr in third ch from hook, 1htr in each st across front to end. (29:**35**:41:**47**:53:**59** sts)

Next row: 2ch, 1htr in each st to end.

Rep last row until 8:**8**:8:**10**:10:**12** rows have been completed, ending at sleeve edge.

Neck shaping:

Next row: 2ch, 1htr across 23:**29**:34:**38**:43:**46** sts, leaving 6:**6**:7:**9**:10:**13** sts unworked.

Next row: 2ch, 1htr in each st to sleeve edge.

Rep last row twice more.

Fasten off.

When working on second front, start with RS facing and make sleeve ch at opposite end to first front.

With RS together, join shoulder seams with ss, working in back loops only.

Sleeve cuffs:

With RS facing, join yarn with ss in first st, make 1ch, turn.

Row 1: 1dc in each row end along edge of sleeve. (23:**23**:27:**29**:33:**35** sts)

Row 2: 1ch, 1dc in next 2 sts, [dc2tog, 1dc in each of next 2:**2**:3:**3**:4:**4** sts] 5 times, 1dc in each st to end. (18:**18**:22:**24**:28:**30** sts)

Row 3: 1ch, 1dc in first and each st to end.

Rep last row 3 times more.

Fasten off.

Finishing

With RS together, join side seams and sleeve seams.

Work shells to fit between markers. Adjust spacings between shells to either miss 1 st or 2 sts. Shells are either made in row ends or sts.

Left front edge:

Place marker halfway down left front edge and work shell edging down left front edge in row ends.

With RS facing, join yarn in first of 6 sts at neck edge of left front, work 4:**4**:4:**4**:5:**6** shells evenly along edge to marker, make another 3:**3**:4:**4**:4:**5** shells evenly to bottom edge, make 1 shell in corner stitch. (8:**8**:9:**9**:10:**11** shells)

Bottom edge:

Divide bottom edge into four by placing marker along bottom edge at each front/back seam and another marker in centre of the back. (3 markers)

Make 3:**3**:4:**4**:5:**5** shells along front bottom edge to first marker, 6:**6**:7:**7**:8:**8** shells along back bottom edge to next marker, 2:**2**:3:**3**:4:**4**

shells along bottom right front edge and 1 shell in next corner. (12:**12**:15:**15**:18:**18** shells)

Right front edge:

Place marker halfway up right front edge. Working in row ends make 3:**3**:4:**4**:4:**5** shells evenly to marker. Make 3:**3**:4:**4**:4:**5** shells evenly to top edge, ending with a dc in last st. (7:**7**:8:**8**:9:**10** shells)

Fasten off. (27:**27**:32:**32**:37:**39** shells)

Neck edging:

Row 1: Join yarn in top of last tr made in shell, 1dc in same st, 1dc in each of next 7 sts, 8:**8**:9:**11**:12:**15** dc across right front neck to shoulder seam, 1dc in each of next

17:**17**:18:**22**:24:**30** sts across back, 8:**8**:9:**11**:12:**15** dc across left front neck, 1dc in each of next 7 sts, 1dc in top of first tr of shell, turn.

Row 2: 1ch, 1dc in first st, 1dc in each st around neck edge.

Row 3: Rep Row 2.

Fasten off.

Using B, C, D, E, F, make 12 (or enough to fit around neck edge) small and light pompoms (see page 65), making sure they are not too thick and sew around collar.

Using shell holes as buttonholes, sew 3 buttons onto front edge.

Frill-edged Cardigan

Something for a special occasion or when you want to go Hollywood and really dress up your baby. This is a really lovely, glamorous little cardigan and an easy pattern.

Materials

Rooster Almerino Baby

→ 3:3:3:4:5 x 50g (1¾oz) balls – approx 375:**375**:375:**500**:625m (409.5:**409.5**:409.5:**546**:682.5yds) – of shade 515 Jellyfish (pale green) (A)

→ 1 x 50g (1¾oz) ball – approx 112.5m (124yds) – of shade 502 Seashell (off white) (B)

→ 3mm (D/3) crochet hook

→ 1m (40in) cream ribbon, cut in half

Abbreviations

ch chain; **beg** beginning; **dc** double crochet; **patt(s)** pattern(s); **rep** repeat; **RS** right side; **sp** space; **ss** slip stitch; **st(s)** stitch(es); **WS** wrong side; **yrh** yarn round hook

Special abbreviations

Patt Row 1 (used on a foundation ch only) 1dc in second ch from hook, insert hook in same ch, pull yarn through (2 loops on hook), *miss 1ch, insert hook in next ch and pull yarn through (3 loops on hook), yrh and pull through all 3 loops, 1ch (1 patt made), insert hook in same ch as last st, pull yarn through; rep from * ending with one complete patt, 1dc in last ch, 1ch, turn

Patt Row 2 1dc in first st, insert hook in ch sp between first st and first patt of last row, pull yarn through (2 loops on hook), *insert hook in ch sp after next patt from previous row, pull yarn through all 3 loops on hook, 1ch (1 patt made), insert hook in same sp as last st, pull yarn through; rep from * to last patt from previous row, work patt over last patt from previous row, 1dc in first dc of previous row, 1ch

Loop st *With yarn over left index finger, insert hook in next st, draw 2 strands through st (take first strand from under index finger and at the same time take second strand from over index finger) pull yarn to tighten loop forming a 2.5cm (1in) loop on index finger. Remove finger from loop, put loop to back of work, yrh and pull through 3 loops on hook (1 loop st made on right side of work)

Size

To fit age: 3–6:**6–12**:12–18:**18–24**:24–36 months

Finished size

Chest	(cm):	52.5	**57.5**	62.5	**67.5**	72.5
	(in):	21	**23**	25	**27**	29
Length	(cm):	22.5	**26.5**	30	**34**	37.5
	(in):	9	**10½**	12	**13½**	15
Sleeve seam	(cm):	16.5	**20**	25	**29**	34
	(in):	6½	**8**	10	**11½**	13½

Tension

11 patt x 9 rows over a 10cm (4in) square working the pattern using a 3mm (D/3) hook.

Back

Using A and starting at lower edge, make 56:**66**:76:**86**:96ch.

Row 1: Work Patt Row 1 to complete 27:**32**:37:**42**:47 patts.

Work using Patt Row 2 until piece measures 14:**16.5**:20:**22.5**:25cm (5½:**6½**:8:**9**:10in)

Divide for sleeves:

Make 32:**38**:44:**50**:56ch for first sleeve.

Drop loop off hook, do not fasten off.

With RS facing, join a separate ball of A in dc at opposite end of last row, make 32:**38**:44:**50**:56ch for second sleeve.

Fasten off.

Pick up dropped loop, turn.

Work Patt Row 1 on 32:**38**:44:**50**:56ch to complete 15:**18**:21:**24**:27 patts, draw up a loop in same ch as last st, miss last ch and 1 dc, draw up a loop between dc and first patt, yrh and through 3 loops on hook, 1ch.

Work in patt across back to last dc, insert hook in same sp as last pattern, miss 1 st, draw up a loop in first ch of 32:**38**:44:**50**:56ch, yrh and pull through all 3 loops on hook, 1ch.

Work 15:**18**:21:**24**:27 patts across ch, 1dc in last ch (59:**65**:71:**77**:83 patts), 1ch, turn.

Work in patt until sleeves measure 9:9:10:10:11.5cm (3½:3½:4:4:4½in) straight up from sleeve ch, 1ch, turn.

Right shoulder and front:

Work 24:**27**:29:**32**:34 patts, 1dc in same sp as last st, 1ch, turn.

Work 2 more rows of 24:**27**:29:**32**:34 patts for shoulder.

Make 9:**13**:17:**19**:25ch for front, turn.

Work 4:**6**:8:**10**:12 patts on chain, plus 1 patt over dc at neck edge.

Continue across front and sleeve in patt. (29:**31**:33:**35**:37 patts)

*Work across 29:**31**:33:**35**:37 patts until sleeve measures 9:**10**:11.5:**12.5**:14cm (3½:**4**:4½:**5**:5½in) from top of shoulder ending centre front edge, 1ch, turn.

Work across 14:**16**:19:**21**:24 patts for front, 1dc in same sp as last st, 1ch, turn.

Work across 14:**16**:19:**21**:24 patts until front measures same as back to sleeve.

Fasten off.*

Left shoulder and front:

Miss 11:**11**:13:**13**:15 patts for back of neck on last row of 59:**65**:71:**77**:83 patts.

Join A in sp before next patt, 1ch, 1dc in same sp.

Work in patt on next 24:**27**:29:**32**:34 patts to end of row.

Work 2 more rows of 24:**27**:29:**32**:34 patts, ending at sleeve edge.

Drop loop off hook, do not fasten off.

Join a separate ball of A at neck edge (beg of last row), make 8:**12**:16:**20**:24ch.

Fasten off.

Pick up loop at sleeve edge, 1ch, turn.

Work across 24:**27**:29:**32**:34 patts, work 1 patt over dc at neck edge, work 4:**6**:8:**10**:12 patts on 8:**12**:16:**20**:24ch. (29:**31**:33:**35**:37 patts)

Working from * to *, complete left front as for right front.

Sew side and sleeve seams.

Frill edging

Front and bottom edging:

Row 1: With RS facing, join B at beg of left front neck edge, work 2dc in each row end along front edge, 3dc in corner, 2dc in each patt along bottom edge, 3dc in next corner, 2dc in each row end along right front edge, 3dc in corner of neck, 1dc in each patt st along right neck edge, finishing at left front neck edge, 1ch, turn.

Row 2: With WS facing, work Loop st in each st around neck, right front, bottom edge, left front, 1ch, turn.

Fasten off.

Row 3: With WS facing, join yarn in first st in right front neck edge, rep Row 2 along right front edge, bottom and up left front edge, finishing at top of left front edge.

Fasten off.

Cuffs

Round 1: With RS facing, join B to cuff edge of sleeve at underarm seam, work 30dc around cuff edge evenly, ss in first dc to join round, turn.

Round 2 (WS facing): 1ch, work Loop st in each st, join with a ss in first 1-ch, do not turn.

Round 3: 1ch, rep Round 2 to end, ss in first 1-ch.

Fasten off.

Finishing

Block cardigan. Sew in ends.

Sew ribbon lengths on either side of neck edge for ties.

Strawberry Kisses Jumper

A very appealing pattern; this warm garment is made using a very soft alpaca/merino wool. When working the pattern rows, place markers in the first and last stitches to help you keep track.

Materials

Rooster Almerino DK

→ 4:4:5:5:6:7 x 50g (1¾oz) balls – approx 450:**450**:562.5:**562.5**:675:**787.5**m (496:**496**:620:**620**:744:**868**yds) – of shade 219 Sandcastle (yellow) (A)

→ 1 x 50g (1¾oz) ball – approx 112.5m (124yds) – of shade 220 Lighthouse (red) (B)

→ Small amounts of shade 201 Cornish (off white) (C) and 207 Gooseberry (green) (D)

→ 3.5mm (E/4) and 3mm (D/4) crochet hooks

→ 1 button

Abbreviations

ch chain; **dc** double crochet; **dec** decrease; **htr** half treble; **inc** increase; **patt** pattern; **rep** repeat; **RS** right side; **ss** slip stitch; **st(s)** stitch(es); **tr** treble; **WS** wrong side; **yrh** yarn round hook

Special abbreviations

Patt A (Row 1 of patt, worked over 5 sts from right to left) Miss 1 st, 1tr in each of next 2 sts, placing hook in front of 2 tr just worked, yrh, insert hook in missed st (from WS to RS), yrh, pull yarn through (3 loops on hook), yrh, pull yarn through 2 loops, yrh, pull yarn through a loop – this is the loop you catch on the next row – (2 loops on hook), yrh, insert hook in fifth st, yrh, pull yarn through (4 loops on hook), yrh, pull yarn through 2 loops, yrh, pull yarn through all 3 loops. Turn work to WS facing, 1 tr in each of third and fourth sts working from back, hook direction front to back

Patt B (Row 2 of patt, worked over 5 sts from right to left) Miss each of next 2 sts, 1tr in third st catching loop from previous row (where central cross is made), keeping hook in front of tr just worked make 1tr in first missed st (from RS to WS), yrh, insert hook in second missed st (from front to back), yrh, pull yarn through (3 loops on hook), yrh, pull yarn through 2 loops (2 loops on hook), yrh, insert hook in fourth st, yrh, pull yarn through (4 loops on hook), yrh, pull yarn through 2 loops, yrh, pull yarn through 3 loops, 1tr in fifth st. Turn work to RS facing. To make fourth point of the cross, 1tr in third st, picking up central loop as before (where central cross is made), turn work back to WS facing

tr2tog (treble 2 together decrease) *yrh, insert hook in next st, yrh, pull yarn through, yrh, pull yarn through 2 loops on hook (2 loops on hook). Without finishing st, rep from * in next st (3 loops on hook), yrh, pull yarn through all 3 loops on hook

tr2tog extra (sts used will vary when decreasing) yrh, insert hook in first st from back to front, yrh, pull yarn through (3 loops on hook), yrh, pull yarn through 2 loops, yrh, pull yarn through 1 loop – this is the loop you catch on the next row – (2 loops on hook), yrh, insert hook in fifth st, yrh, pull yarn through, yrh pull yarn through 2 loops, yrh pull yarn through all 3 loops

tr2tog over (sts used will vary when decreasing) yrh, insert hook in second st 2 from front to back, yrh, pull yarn through (3 loops on hook), yrh, pull yarn through 2 loops (2 loops on hook), yrh, insert hook in fourth st, yrh, pull yarn through (4 loops on hook), yrh, pull yarn through 2 loops, yrh, pull yarn through all 3 loops

Size

To fit age: 0–3:**3–6**:6–12:**12–18**:18–24:**24–36** months

Finished size

Chest	(cm):	50	55	60	65	70	75
	(in):	20	22	24	26	28	30
Length	(cm):	32.5	37.5	42.5	47.5	52.5	57.5
	(in):	13	15	17	19	21	23
Sleeve seam	(cm):	12.5	16.5	20	25	27.5	30
	(in):	5	6½	8	10	11	12

Tension

2¾ patterns x 10 rows over a 10cm (4in) square using a 3.5mm (E/4) hook.

Back

Using 3.5mm (E/4) hook and A, make
50:**55**:60:**65**:70:**75**ch.

Row 1: 1dc in second ch from hook, 1dc in
each chain to end. (49:**54**:59:**64**:69:**74** sts)

Row 2: 1dc in first st, 1ch (counts as 1htr), 1htr
in each st to end.

Row 3 (row 1 of pattern): 1dc in first st, 2ch
(counts as 1tr), 1tr in each of next 3 sts, *Patt
A, 1tr in each of next 4 sts; rep from * to end.

Row 4 (row 2 of pattern): 1dc in first st, 2ch
(counts as 1tr), 1tr in each of next 3 sts, *Patt
B, 1tr in each of next 4 sts; rep from *to end.

Rep Rows 3–4 another 8:**10**:12:**14**:16:**18**
times more.

Shape for armholes:

Row 21:**25**:29:**33**:37:**41**: Ss in first 3 sts, 1dc in
next st, 2ch (counts as tr), Patt A, *1tr in each
of next 4 sts, Patt A; rep from * to last 4 sts, 1tr
in next st, turn. (43:**48**:53:**58**:63:**68** sts)

Row 22:**26**:30:**34**:38:**42** (dec row Patt B): 1dc
in first st, 2ch (counts as 1tr), miss next 2 sts,
1tr in third st catching loop from previous row
(where central cross is made), keeping hook
in front of tr just worked tr2tog using first and
second sts (inserting hook from RS to WS),
tr2tog using fourth and fifth sts. Turn work to
RS facing. To make fourth point of cross 1tr in
third st picking up central loop as before
(where central cross is made), turn work back
to WS facing, 1tr in each of next 4 sts, *Patt B,
1tr in each of next 4 sts; rep from * to last 6
sts, miss first and second sts, 1tr in third st
catching loop from previous row (where
central cross is made). Keeping hook in front
of tr just worked tr2tog using first and second
sts (inserting hook from RS to WS), tr2tog

using fourth and fifth sts, turn work to RS facing. To make fourth point of cross 1tr in third st picking up central loop as before (where central cross is made). Turn work back to WS facing, 1tr in last st. (41:**46**:51:**56**:61:**66** sts)

Row 23:27:31:35:39:43 (dec row, Patt A worked on 4 sts): 1dc in first st, 2ch (counts as 1tr), miss 3 sts, 1tr in next st, turn work to WS facing, 1 tr in each of first and second sts, turn work to RS facing, 1tr in each of next 4 sts, *Patt A, 1tr in each of next 4 sts; rep from * to last 5 sts, miss first st, 1tr in second st, tr2tog extra using first st and fourth st, turn work to WS facing, 1tr in third st, turn work to RS facing, 1tr in last st. (39:**44**:49:**54**:59:**64** sts)

Row 24:28:32:36:40:44 (dec row, Patt B worked on 3 sts): 1dc in first st, 1ch, miss 1 st, 1tr in third st (counts as 1tr), turn work to RS facing, 1tr in second st, *1tr in each of next 4 sts, Patt B; rep from * to last 4 sts, miss first 2 sts, 1tr in third st (no extra loop to catch this time), tr2tog over using first and last st. (37:**42**:47:**52**:57:**62** sts)

Row 25:29:33:37:41:45 (dec row): 1dc in first st, 2ch (counts as 1tr), tr2tog, 1tr in each of next 4 sts, *Patt A, 1tr in each of next 4 sts; rep from * to last 7 sts, 1tr in each of next 4 sts, tr2tog, 1tr in last st. (35:**40**:45:**50**:55:**60** sts)

Row 26:30:34:38:42:46: 1dc in first st, 2ch (counts as 1tr), 1tr in each of next 5 sts, *Patt B, 1tr in each of next 4 sts; rep from * to last 2 sts, 1tr in each of next 2 sts.

Row 27:31:35:39:43:47: 1dc in first st, 2ch (counts as 1tr), 1tr in each of next 5 sts, *Patt A, 1tr in each of next 4 sts; rep from *to last 2 sts, 1tr in each of next 2 sts.

Row 28:32:36:40:44:48: Rep Row 26:30:34:38:42:46.

Row 29:33:37:41:45:49: Rep Row 27:31:35:39:43:47.

Row 30:34:38:42:46:50: Rep Row 26:30:34:38:42:46.

Rep Rows 27–26 another 0:**1**:2:**3**:4:**4** times more.

Right shoulder:

Rows 31–33:36–38:40–42:46–48:52–54:58–60: 1dc in first st, 2ch, 1tr in each of next 5:**7**:9:**11**:13:**15** sts.

Fasten off.

Left shoulder (incl flap over):

Row 31:36:40:46:52:58: With RS facing, join yarn with ss, 2ch in 6th:**8th**:10th:**12th**:14th:**16th** st from outside edge, 1tr in each of next 5:**7**:9:**11**:13:**15** sts, turn.

Rows 32–36:37–41:41–45:49–51:52–56:58–62: 1dc in first st, 2ch (counts as 1tr), 1tr in each of next 5:**7**:9:**11**:13:**15** sts.

Fasten off.

Front

Work as Back to Row 25:**29**:31:**35**:39:**43**.

Right front neck:

Row 26:30:32:36:40:44 (dec row Patt B): 1dc in first st, 2ch (counts as 1tr), 1tr in each of next 5 sts, Patt B, 1tr in next 1:**3**:5:**7**:9:**11** sts (neck edge), turn. (12:**14**:16:**18**:20:**22** sts)

Row 27:31:33:37:41:45 (dec row Patt A): 1dc in first 1:**3**:5:**7**:9:**11** sts, 2ch (counts as 1tr), miss next st, tr2tog using second and third sts, keeping hook in front of tr just worked, tr2tog extra using first and fifth sts, turn work to WS facing, 1tr in each of third and fourth sts, 1tr in

each of next 6 sts. (11:**13**:15:**17**:19:**21** sts)

Row 28:32:34:38:42:46 (dec row Patt B): 1dc in first st, 2ch (counts as 1tr), 1tr in each of next 5 sts, miss 2 sts, 1tr in next st catching loop from previous row, 1tr in first st, tr2tog over using second and fourth sts, turn work to RS facing. To make fourth point of cross 1tr in third st picking up central loop as before (where central cross is made), turn work back to WS facing, 1tr in each st to end. (10:**12**:14:**16**:18:**20** sts)

Row 29:33:35:39:43:47 (dec row Patt A): 1dc in first st, 2ch (counts as 1tr), miss 2 sts, 1tr in next 1:**3**:5:**7**:9:**11** sts, turn work to WS facing, tr2tog using first and second sts, 1tr in each of next 6 sts. (9:**11**:13:**15**:17:**19** sts)

Row 30:34:36:40:44:48: 1dc in first st, 2ch, 1tr in each of next 5 sts, tr2tog, 1 tr in last st. (8:**10**:12:**14**:16:**18** sts)

Row 31:35:37:41:45:49: 1dc in first st, 2ch, tr2tog, 1tr in each of next 5 sts. (7:**9**:11:**13**:15:**17** sts)

Row 32:36:38:42:46:50: 1dc in first st, 2ch, 1tr in each of next 4 sts, tr2tog, 1tr in each st to end. (6:**8**:10:**12**:14:**16** sts)

Row 33:37:39:43:47:51: 1dc in first st, 2ch, 1tr in each st to end. (6:**8**:10:**12**:14:**16** sts)

Fasten off.

Left front neck:

With WS facing, join yarn in 12th:**14th**:16th:**18th**:20th:**22nd** st from left.

Row 26:30:32:36:40:44 (dec row Patt B): 3ch (counts as 1:**3**:5:**7**:9:**11**tr), Patt B, 1tr in each of next 6 sts. (12:**14**:16:**18**:20:**22** sts)

Row 27:31:33:37:41:45 (dec row Patt A): 1dc in first st, 2ch (counts as 1tr), 1tr in each of next 5 sts, miss 1 st, 1tr in each of second and third sts, keeping hook in front of tr just worked, tr2tog extra using first and fifth sts, turn work to WS facing, 1tr in third st, tr2tog over using fourth and last st. (11:**13**:15:**17**:19:**21** sts)

Row 28:32:34:38:42:46 (dec row Patt B): 1dc in first st, 2ch (counts as 1tr), miss 1 st, 1tr in second st catching loop from previous row, tr2tog over using first and fourth sts, turn work to RS facing. To make fourth point of cross 1tr in second st picking up central loop as before (where central cross is made), turn work back to WS facing, 1tr in each of next 6 sts. (10:**12**:14:**16**:18:**20** sts)

Row 29:33:35:39:43:47 (dec row Patt A): 1dc in first st, 2ch (counts as 1tr), 1tr in each of next 5 sts, tr2tog extra using first and third sts, turn work to WS facing, 1tr in first st, tr2tog over using second and last st. (9:**11**:13:**15**:17:**19** sts)

Row 30:34:36:40:44:48: 1dc in first st, 2ch, tr2tog, 1tr in each of next 6 sts. (8:**10**:12:**14**:16:**18** sts)

Row 31:35:37:41:45:49: 1dc in first st, 2ch (counts as 1tr), tr2tog, 1tr in each st to end. (7:**9**:11:**13**:15:**17** sts)

Row 32:36:38:42:46:50: 1dc in first st, 2ch, tr2tog, 1tr in each of next 4 sts. (6:**8**:10:**12**:14:**16** sts)

Row 33:37:39:43:47:51: 1dc in first st, 2ch, 1tr in each st to end. (6:**8**:10:**12**:14:**16** sts)
    Fasten off.

Sleeves (make 2)

Using 3.5mm (E/4) hook and A, make 28:**30**:32:**34**:36:**38**ch.

Row 1: 1dc in second ch from hook, 1dc in each ch to end.

Row 2: 1dc in first st, 1ch (counts as 1htr), 1htr in each st to end.

Row 3: 1dc in first st, 2ch (counts as 1tr), 1tr in next 1:**2**:3:**4**:5:**6** sts, Patt A, *1tr in each of next 4 sts, Patt A; rep from * once more, 1tr in each of last 2:**3**:4:**5**:6:**7** sts.

Row 4: 1dc in first st, 2ch (counts as 1tr), 1tr in next 1:**2**:3:**4**:5:**6** sts, Patt B, *1tr in each of next 4 sts, Patt B; rep from * once more, 1tr in each of last 2:**3**:4:**5**:6:**7** sts.

Inc rows:

Row 5: 1dc in first st, 2ch (counts as 1tr), 2tr in next st, 1tr in each of next 0:**1**:2:**3**:4:**5** sts, *Patt A, 1tr in each of next 4 sts; rep from * once more, Patt A, 1tr in each st to end.

Row 6: 1dc in first st, 2ch (counts as 1tr), 2tr in next st, 1tr in each of next 0:**1**:2:**3**:4:**5** sts, *Patt B, 1tr in each of next 4 sts; rep from * once more, Patt B, 1tr in each st to end.

Rows 7–16: Rep Rows 5–6 until there are 8:**9**:10:**11**:12:**13** tr at end of each row.

Row 17: 1ss in each of first 3 sts, 1dc in next 1:**2**:3:**4**:5:**6** sts, 2ch (counts as 1tr), 1tr in each of next 4 sts, Patt A, *1tr in each of next 4 sts, Patt A; rep from * once more, 1tr in each of next 5:**6**:7:**8**:9:**10** sts, turn.

    Work a further 0:**4**:8:**12**:16:**20** rows without shaping.

Dec rows:

Row 18:22:26:30:34:38: 1dc in first st, 2ch (counts as 1tr), tr2tog, 1tr in each of next 2 sts, Patt B, *1tr in each of next 4 sts; rep from * once more, 1tr in each of next 2 sts, tr2tog, 1tr in last st.

Row 19:23:27:31:35:39: 1dc in first st, 2ch (counts as 1tr), tr2tog, 1tr in next st, Patt A, *1tr in each of next 4 sts, Patt A; rep from * once more, 1tr in next st, tr2tog, 1tr in last st.

Row 20:24:28:32:36:40: 1dc in first st, 2ch (counts as 1tr), tr2tog, Patt B, *1tr in each of next 4 sts, Patt B; rep from * once more, tr2tog, 1tr in last st.

Row 21:25:29:33:37:41: 1dc in first st, [1ch, 1tr] (counts as tr2tog) Patt A, *1tr in each of next 4 sts, Patt A; rep from * once more, tr2tog.

Row 22:26:30:34:38:42: 1dc in first st, 2ch (counts as 1tr), Patt B, *1tr in each of next 4 sts, Patt B; rep from * once more, 1tr in last st.

Row 23:27:31:35:39:43: 1dc in first st, 2ch (counts as 1tr), Patt A, *1tr in each of next 4 sts, Patt A; rep from * once more, 1tr in last st.

Row 24:28:32:36:40:44: 1dc in first st, 2ch (counts as 1tr), Patt B, *1tr in each of next 4 sts, Patt B; rep from * once more, 1tr in last st.

Row 25:29:33:37:41:45: 1dc in first st, 2ch (counts as 1tr), miss next st, tr2tog using second and third sts, keeping hook in front of tr just worked tr2tog extra using first and fifth sts, turn work to WS facing, 1tr in third and fourth sts, 1tr in next st, tr2tog, 1tr in next st, Patt A, miss 1 st, 1tr in second and third sts, keeping hook in front of tr just worked, tr2tog extra using first and fifth sts, turn work to WS facing, tr2tog using third and fourth sts, 1tr in last st.
    Fasten off.

Finishing

With RS together, sew front and back together (left shoulder has more rows for button flap).
    Sew sleeve seams.

Neck edge:

With RS facing, join yarn at left front shoulder

edge, 2ch, 1htr in each st (picking up even number of sts on both sides of neck edge). Work to position of buttonhole, 2ch, miss 2 sts, continue in htr to end, turn, 1ch, 1dc in first st, 1dc in each st to end.

Sew button in place.

Strawberries (make enough to go around bottom edge between crosses)

Using 3mm (D/4) hook and B, make 2ch, 1dc in second ch from hook, 1ch, turn and make next row on side edge.

2dc in first st, 1ch, turn. (2 sts)

2dc in each st, 1ch, turn. (4 sts)

1dc in next st, 2dc in next st, 1dc in next st, 2dc in next st, 1ch, turn. (6 sts)

1dc in first st, 2dc in next st, 1dc in each of next 2 sts, 2dc in next st, 1dc in next st. (8 sts)

Fasten off leaving a long tail.

Fold sides together and hand sew along side and top of strawberry, folding and sewing in tip to neaten. Sew in ends.

Using yarn needle and C, embroider 3 small seeds on each strawberry.

Leaves (make 1 for each strawberry)

With RS facing and using 3mm (D/4) hook and D, insert hook through top sts (second from right) at top right side of strawberry and join yarn.

*Make 3ch, ss to base of ch, ss in next st; rep from * once more.

Fasten off. Sew in ends.

Sew strawberries around bottom edge between crosses.

CHAPTER TWO

Stepping Out

✿✿✿✿✿✿✿✿✿✿✿✿✿✿✿✿✿✿✿✿✿✿✿✿✿✿✿✿✿✿✿✿✿

 Improver

Lilac Bootees

The cutest little slippers with a
strap to keep them in place.

Materials

Rooster Almerino Baby

➜ 1 x 50g (1¾oz) ball – 125m (136yds) – of
  each of shade 511 Anemone (purple) (A)
  and 512 Horizon (lilac) (B)
➜ 3mm (D/3) crochet hook
➜ 2 buttons

Abbreviations

ch chain; **dc** double crochet; **htr** half treble;
rep repeat; **sp** space; **ss** slip stitch;
st(s) stitch(es); **tr** treble

Size

To fit age: Newborn baby

Finished size

Length: approx 9cm (3½in)

Bootee (make 2)

Using A, make 12ch.

Round 1: 1dc in second ch from hook, 1dc in each of next 9ch, 6dc in last ch.

Working on other side of chain, 1dc in each ch to last ch, 2dc in last ch, join with ss in first st.

Round 2: 1ch, 1dc in each of next 6 sts, 1htr in each of next 5 sts, *2htr in next st, 1htr in next st; rep from * once more, 2htr in next st, 1htr in each of next 5 sts, 1dc in each of next 7 sts, join with ss in first ch.

Round 3: 1ch, 1dc in next st, 2dc in next st, 1dc in each of next 4 sts, 1htr in each of next 6 sts, *2htr in next st, 1htr in next st; rep from * twice more, 2htr in next st, 1htr in each of next 6 sts, 1dc in each of next 4 sts, 2dc in next st, 1dc in next st, 2dc in last st, join with ss in first ch.

Round 4: 2ch, 2htr in next st, 1htr in each of next 16 sts, *2htr in next st, 1htr in next st; rep from * once more, 2htr in next st, 1htr in each of next 16 sts, 2htr in next st, 1htr in last st, join with ss in top of first ch.

Join in B, do not fasten off A.

Round 5: Using B, 2ch, 1htr in each st to end, join with ss in top of first ch.

Fasten off B.

Round 6: Using A, 1ch, 1dc in each st to end, ss in top of first ch, turn.

Begin working in rows:

Row 1: 1ch, miss first st, 1dc in next st, miss 1 st, 1dc in each of next 14 sts, *miss 1 st, 1dc in each of next 4 sts; rep from * twice more, miss 1 st, 1dc in each of next 14 sts, miss 1 st, join with ss in top of first ch.

Row 2: 1ch, 1dc in each of next 14 sts, *miss 1 st, 1dc in each of next 3 sts; rep from * twice more, miss 1 st, 1dc in each st to end.

Row 3: 1ch, 1dc in each of next 15 sts, *miss 1 st, 1dc in each of next 4 sts; rep from * once more, miss 1 st, 1dc in each st to end.

Place a marker st in the centre front st.

Left-hand side:

Row 1: 1ch, 1dc in each st to centre point, miss centre st, turn.

Row 2: 1ch, miss 1 st, 1dc in each st to end, turn.

Row 3: 1ch, 1dc in each st to last 4 sts, miss 1 st, 1dc in next st, miss 1 st, 1dc in last st, turn.

Row 4: 1ch, miss 1 st, 1dc in each st to end, turn.

Row 5: 1ch, 1dc in each st to last 2 sts, miss 1 st, 1dc in last st, turn.

Row 6: 1ch, miss 1 st, 1dc in each st to end, turn.

Row 7: 1ch, 1dc in each st to end.

Fasten off.

Right-hand side:

Join A to st next to centre front (do not use centre stitch).

Row 1: 1ch, 1dc in each st, join with ss to centre back, turn.

Row 2: 1ch, 1dc in each st to last 4 sts, miss 1 st, 1dc, miss 1 st, 1dc, turn.

Row 3: 1ch, miss 1 st, 1dc in next st, 1dc in each st to end, turn.

Row 4: 1ch, 1dc in each st to last 2 sts, miss 1 st, 1dc in last st, turn.

Row 5: 1ch, miss 1 st, 1dc in each st to end, turn.

Rows 6–7: 1ch, 1dc in each st to end.

Fasten off.

Join B in centre back st, work 1dc around edge of bootee opening including centre front stitch.

Fasten off.

Straps (make 2)

Using A, make 11ch.

Row 1: 1dc in second ch from hook, 1dc in each st to end, turn.

Row 2: 1ch, 1dc in each st to end.

Row 3: 1ch, 1dc in each of next 7 sts, 2ch, miss 2 sts, 1dc in each st to end.

Row 4: 1ch, 1dc in each st (including 1dc in 2-ch) to end.

Fasten off.

Finishing

Sew strap on left for right bootee and on right for left bootee. Sew on buttons to match straps.

Ribbon Hat

This is a perfect first baby hat. It's so easy to make and the ribbon and flower add a delicate and stylish look.

Materials

Rooster Almerino Baby

→ 1 x 50g (1¾oz) ball – approx 125m (136yds) – of shade 502 Seashell (off white) (A)

→ Small amount of shade 512 Horizon (lilac) (B)

→ Small amount of shade 511 anemone (purple) (C)

→ 3mm (D/3) crochet hook

→ Approx 30cm (12in) of 1cm (½in) wide lilac ribbon

Abbreviations

ch chain; **dc** double crochet; **htr** half treble; **rep** repeat; **sp** space; **ss** slip stitch; **st(s)** stitch(es); **tr** treble

Size

To fit age: Newborn baby

Finished size

Circumference: 37.5cm (15in)

Tension

24 sts x 15 rows over a 10cm (4in) square working pattern using a 3mm (D/3) hook.

Hat

Using A, make 4ch, ss in first ch to form a ring.

Round 1: 5ch, *1tr, 2ch in ring; rep from * 4 more times, ss in third of 5-ch, ss in fourth of same 5-ch.

Round 2: 5ch, *1tr in first ch sp, 2ch, *[1tr, 2ch, 1tr] in next ch sp; rep from * to end, ss in third of first 5-ch, ss in fourth of same 5-ch.

Round 3: 5ch, 1tr in first ch sp, *2ch, 1tr in next ch sp, 2ch, [1tr, 2ch, 1tr] in next ch sp; rep from * to end, ss in third of 5-ch, ss in fourth of same 5-ch.

Round 4: 5ch, 1tr in first ch sp, *2ch, 1tr in next ch sp, 2ch, 1tr in next ch sp. 2ch, [1tr, 2ch, 1tr] in next ch sp; rep from * to end, ss in third of 5-ch, ss in fourth of same 5-ch.

Round 5: 5ch, 1tr in first ch sp, *2ch, 1tr in next ch sp, 2ch, 1tr in next ch sp, 2ch, 1tr in next ch sp, 2ch, [1tr, 2ch, 1tr] in next ch sp; rep from * to end, ss in third of 5-ch, ss in fourth of same 5-ch.

Round 6: 5ch, 1tr in first ch sp, *2ch, 1tr in next ch sp, 2ch, 1tr in next ch sp, 2ch, 1tr in next ch sp, 2ch, 1tr in next ch sp, 2ch, [1tr, 2ch, 1tr] in next ch sp; rep from * to end, ss in third of 5-ch, ss in fourth of same 5-ch.

Rounds 7–16: 5ch, 1tr, 1ch in each ch sp around (36 sts), ss in third of 5-ch, ss in fourth of same 5-ch.

Round 17: 1ch, *2dc in next ch sp, 1dc in next ch sp, 3ch, ss in first ch, 1dc in same ch sp, 2dc in next ch sp, 3ch, ss in first ch; rep from *

to end, ss in first ch to join round.

Fasten off.

Flowers

Using B, make 4ch, ss in first ch to make a ring.

Round 1: [3ch, 1dc into middle of 4-ch] 5 times (5 holes for petals), ss in first ch.

Round 2: [1dc, 1htr, 2tr, 1htr, 1dc] in each ch sp, ss into base of first 3-ch from previous round.

Change to C.

Round 3: [Place the hook through centre hole from front to back and back through middle hole of any petal, make 1dc, 3ch] 5 times.

Round 4: [1dc, 1tr, 1dc] in each ch sp, ss into base of first dc.

Fasten off.

Finishing

Sew in ends.

Weave ribbon around holes in stitches. Sew ends of ribbon together to attach.

Stitch flower to hat.

Beanie Hat

A really simple beanie hat pattern decorated with a pretty boat motif. Always use a very soft yarn if making something that will be worn on a baby's head.

Hat

Using A and 3mm (D/3) hook, make 4ch, ss in first ch to make a ring.

Round 1: 2ch, make 8htr into ring, join with ss in first 2-ch. (8 sts)

Round 2: 2ch, 1htr in same st, 2htr in each st to end, join with ss in first 2-ch. (16 sts)

Round 3: 2ch, 1htr in same st, *1htr in next st, 2htr in next st; rep from * to end, join with ss in first 2-ch. (24 sts)

Round 4: Rep Round 3. (36 sts)

Round 5: 2ch, 1htr in same st, *1htr in each of next 2 sts, 2htr in next st; rep from * to last 2 sts, 1htr in last 2 sts, join with ss in first 2-ch. (48 sts)

Round 6: 2ch, 1htr in same st, *1htr in each of next 7 sts, 2htr in next st; rep from * to last 7 sts, 1htr in each st to end, join with ss in first 2-ch. (54 sts)

Round 7: 2ch, 1htr in same st, *1htr in each of next 8 sts, 2htr in next st; rep from * to last 8 sts, 1htr in each st to end, join with ss in first 2-ch. (60 sts)

Rounds 8–14: 2ch, 1htr in each st to end, join with ss in first 2-ch.

Join in B.

Round 15: 1dc in each st to end, join with ss.

Join in C.

Round 16: 1dc in each st to end, join with ss.

Fasten off.

Boat motif base

Using red and 2.5mm (C/2) hook, make 9ch, 1dc in next ch from hook, 1htr in next st, 1tr in next st, 1dtr in next st, 1tr in next st, 1htr in next st, 1dc, ss in first ch.

Fasten off.

Boat motif sails

Using white and 2.5mm (C/2) hook, make 11ch, make 1dc in second ch from hook, 1dc in next ch, 1htr in next ch, 1tr in each of next 2ch, 1dtr in next ch, 1trtr in next ch, 1quad tr in next ch.

Fasten off.

Working on other side of ch just worked with WS facing, join blue in underside of second dc, 1dc in next ch, 1htr in next ch, 1tr in next ch, 1dtr in next ch, 1trtr in next ch 1quad tr in next ch, 6ch, join with ss in next ch.

Fasten off.

Finishing

Sew boat motif sail onto boat base using yarn needle and attaching to the centre bottom chain of the straighter edge of the bottom of boat.

Sew boat motif onto hat.

Materials

Rooster Almerino Baby

➜ 1 x 50g (1¾oz) ball – approx 125m (136yds) – each of shade 502 Seashell (off white) (A), 207 Gooseberry (green) (B), 205 Glace (pale blue) (C)

➜ Scraps of red, white and blue

➜ 3mm (D/3) and 2.5mm (C/2) crochet hooks

Abbreviations

ch chain; **dc** double crochet; **dtr** double treble; **htr** half treble; **rep** repeat; **sp** space; **ss** slip stitch; **st(s)** stitch(es); **tr** treble; **trtr** triple treble; **quad tr** quadruple treble

Size

To fit age: 3–6 months

Finished size

Circumference: 36cm (14in)

Tension

18 sts x 13 rows over a 10cm (4in) square working in half treble using a 3mm (D/3) hook.

Brimmed Baby Hat

A very pretty and cute hat for a toddler. This is made in a fine wool/silk yarn, which is very soft and easy to wear. Perfect for both keeping the sun off baby's head or keeping nice and warm in the winter.

Hat

Using 2.5mm (C/2) hook and A, make 5ch, join with ss into first ch to make a ring.

Round 1: 12tr into ring.

Round 2: *1dc into first tr, 2dc into second tr; rep from * to end. (18 sts)

Round 3: *1dc in first st, 2dc in next st; rep from * to end. (24 sts)

Cont increasing in this way, making 2dc in first of 2 sts below and having one more stitch between increases, until work measures 7.5cm (3in) from centre of crown to edge.

Next round: 1dc in each st. (114 sts)

Next round: 1ch, *dc2tog, 1ch; rep from * to end. (115 sts)

Next round: *Dc2tog (draw yarn through st at each side of group below), 1ch; rep from * to end. (114 sts)

Rep last round seven more times.

Next round: 1dc in each st.

Make brim:

Round 32: *1dc in each of next 5 sts, 2dc in next st; rep from * to end. (133 sts)

Rounds 33–36: 1dc in each st.

Round 37: As Round 32. (155 sts)

Rounds 38–40: 1dc in each st.

Round 41: *1dc in each of next 7 sts, 2dc in next st; rep from * to end. (173 sts)

Rounds 42–43: 1dc in each st.

Fasten off.

Flowers (make 3)

Using A and 4mm (F/5) hook, make 6ch, join with ss into first chain to make a ring.

Make 16dc into ring, join with ss.

Fasten off.

Join B into fastened off st.

*3ch, 1tr into next 2 sts, 3ch, ss into next st; rep from * four times (5 petals).

Fasten off.

Finishing

Sew in ends on hat.

Using a yarn needle, weave around the centre hole of flower to close and tighten; sew in ends.

Position flowers as required and stitch to hat.

Materials

Fyberspates Scrumptious 4-ply

→ 1 x 100g (3½oz) skein – approx 365m (399yds) – of shade 304 Water (grey) (A)

Rooster Almerino DK

→ Small amount of shade 211 Brighton Rock (bright pink) (B)

→ 2.5mm (C/2) and 4mm (F/5) crochet hooks

Abbreviations

ch chain; **cont** continue; **dc** double crochet; **dc2tog** (double crochet 2 together decrease) insert hook in next st, yrh, pull yarn through (2 loops on hook). Without finishing st, insert hook in next st, yrh, pull yarn through (3 loops on hook), yrh, pull yarn through all 3 loops on hook; **rep** repeat; **ss** slip stitch; **st(s)** stitch(es); **tr** treble; **yrh** yarn round hook

Size

To fit age: 12–36 months

Finished size

Circumference: approx 42.5–45cm (17–18in)

Ophelia Buggy Blanket

Just large enough to tuck in the toes, this is the perfect size for a buggy or car seat blanket. The colour combinations are light and bright, which make it a suitable blanket for either a boy or a girl.

Blanket

Change colour on each row.

Using first colour, make 83ch.

Row 1: 1tr in 2nd ch from hook, 1tr in next ch, *1tr in each of next 3 ch, tr3tog over next 3ch, 1tr in next 3-ch, 3tr in next ch; rep from * ending last rep with 2tr in last ch, turn.

Row 2: 3ch, 1tr in first st, *1tr in each of next 3 sts, tr3tog over next 3 sts, 1tr in each of next 3 sts, 3tr in next st; rep from * ending last rep with 2tr in top of turning chain, turn.

Change colour.

Rep Row 2 another 48 times more, making a total of 50 rows.

Fasten off.

Edging

Round 1: With RS facing, join A in fasten off st.

Materials

Rooster Almerino DK

→ 1 x 50g (1¾oz) ball – approx 112.5m (124yds) – each of shade 201 Cornish (off white) (A), 208 Ocean (blue-green) (B), 211 Brighton Rock (bright pink) (C), 205 Glace (pale blue), 203 Strawberry Cream (pale pink), 207 Gooseberry (green), 210 Custard (yellow), 209 Smoothie (Orange), 214 Damson (dark purple), 204 Grape (purple), 215 Lilac Sky (lilac)

→ 4.5mm (G/6) crochet hook

Abbreviations

ch chain; **dc** double crochet; **htr** half treble; **rep** repeat; **RS** right side; **ss** slip stitch; **st(s)** stitch(es); **tr** treble; **yrh** yarn round hook

Special abbreviation

tr3tog (treble 3 together decrease) *yrh, insert hook in next st, yrh, pull yarn through, yrh, pull yarn through 2 loops on hook (2 loops on hook). Without finishing st, rep from * in each of next 2 sts (4 loops on hook), yrh, pull yarn through all 4 loops on hook

Finished size

Approx 50 x 62.5cm (20 x 25in)

Tension

15 sts x 8 rows over a 10cm (4in) square working treble using a 4.5mm (G/6) hook.

Side 1 (Top):

1ch, 1dc in each of next 2 sts, 1htr in each of next 2 sts, 1tr in each of next 3 sts, 1htr in each of next 2 sts, *1dc in next 3 sts, 1htr in each of next 2 sts, 1tr in each of next 3 sts, 1htr in each of next 2 sts; rep from * to last 2 sts, 1dc in next st, 4dc in corner st.

Side 2:

*Make 2dc in each colour down side, 4dc in corner st.

Side 3:

Working on bottom chain of Row 1 of blanket, 1tr in each of next 2 sts, 1htr in each of next 2 sts; rep from * from Side 1 to last 6 sts, 1dc in each of next 3 sts, 1htr in each of next 2 sts, 1tr in next st, 4dc in corner st.

Side 4:

Rep Side 2 to last st, make 4dc in corner st, ss in first ch from Side 1.

   Fasten off.

Round 2: Using B, make 1dc in each st around blanket, making 4dc in each corner st, join with a ss in first st.

Round 3: Rep Round 2.

   Fasten off.

Pompoms (make 4)

Using C, wrap the yarn around three or four fingers approx 80 times. Gently slide the yarn off your fingers and tie a knot in the centre very securely. The pompom will now have loops on either side of the knot. Cut all the loops; trim and fluff the pompom into shape.

Finishing

Sew in ends.

   Sew one pompom onto each corner of the blanket.

Baby Mittens

A delicious mix of supersoft merino wool and silk – perfect to keep little fingers warm – these mittens are made using a traditional shell pattern with a little shell edging and tied with a pretty ribbon. They look very special but this is a really quick and easy pattern.

Abbreviations

ch chain; **dc** double crochet; **htr** half treble; **rep** repeat; **sp** space; **ss** slip stitch; **st(s)** stitch(es); **tr** treble

Size

To fit age: 0–6 months

Finished size

Length: approx 9cm (3½in)

Materials

Fyberspates Scrumptious 4-ply

→ 1 x 100g (3½oz) skein – approx 365m (399yds) – of shade 310 Natural (ecru) or 306 Baby Pink (pink)

→ 1m (40in) narrow blue or pink ribbon

→ 2.5mm (C/2) crochet hook

Mittens (make 2)

Make 4ch, ss in first ch to make a ring.

Round 1: 3ch (counts as 1tr), 11tr in ring, join with ss in top of first 3-ch. (12 sts)

Round 2: 3ch, 1tr in first st, 2tr in each st to end, join with ss in top of first 3-ch. (24 sts)

Round 3: 3ch, 4tr in same st as 3ch, *miss 1 st, 1dc in next st, miss 1 st, 5tr in next st; rep from * to end, join with ss in base of 3-ch from previous round.

Round 4: Ss in each of next 2 sts, 1ch, *5tr in next dc from previous round, 1dc in middle st of 5-tr shell, 5tr in next dc from previous round; rep from * to end, join with ss in top of first 1-ch.

Round 5: 3ch, 4tr in same st as 3-ch, *1dc in middle st of 5-tr shell, 5tr in next dc from previous round; rep from * to end, join with ss in top of first tr.

Insert st marker at beginning of next round.

Round 6: Rep Round 4.

Round 7: Rep Round 5.

Round 8: Rep Round 4.

Round 9: 2ch, * miss next 2 sts, 1htr in next st; rep from * to end, join with ss in top of first 2-ch.

Round 10: 2ch, *2htr in next sp, 1htr in next dc, ss in top of first 2-ch.

Round 11: *1dc in next st, miss 1 st, 5tr in next st, miss 1 st; rep from * to end, join in first dc with ss.

Finishing

Sew in ends.

Thread ribbon through spaces around top and tie a bow.

Squares

Using dc

CC colou

following

Finishin

Lay squar

across by

are arran

Using

strips tog

Edging:

Round 1:

blanket, r

each st al

corner st

st along e

ss into firs

Round 2:

next corn

twice mo

corner, ss

Round 3:

next corn

more, 1tr

corner, e

ch, ss into

Fasten

Materials

Rooster Almerino DK

→ 1 x 50g (1¾oz) ball – approx 112.5m (124yds) – each of shade 207 Gooseberry (green) (A) and 201 Cornish (off white) (B)

→ 3.5mm (E/4) crochet hook

Abbreviations

ch chain; **dc** double crochet; **htr** half treble; **rep** repeat; **ss** slip stitch; **st(s)** stitch(es); **yrh** yarn round hook

Special abbreviations

Cl (Cluster) yrh, insert hook in st, yrh, pull yarn through, yrh, insert hook in same st, yrh, pull yarn through, yrh, insert hook in same st, yrh, pull yarn through, yrh (7 loops on hook), pull yarn through all 7 loops on hook, yrh, 1ch (1 cluster made)

htr2tog (half treble 2 together decrease) *yrh, insert hook in next st, yrh, pull yarn through (3 loops on hook). Without finishing st, rep from * in next st (5 loops on hook), yrh, pull yarn through all 5 loops on hook

Size

To fit age: approx 12–36 months

Finished size

Length from crown to edge: 17.5cm (7in)
Circumference: 45–50cm (18–20in)

Pompom Hat

This very cute hat is made with super soft alpaca and merino mix so it will not irritate delicate skin. It's such an easy hat to crochet that it can be made over one evening.

Hat

Using A, make 76ch.

Row 1: 1dc in next ch from hook, 1dc in each ch to end.

Rows 2–3: 1ch, 1dc in each st to end.

Row 4: 1ch, 1dc in each of next 5 sts, 2dc in next st, *1dc in each of next 4 sts, 2dc in next st; rep from * to last 5 sts, 1dc in each of next 5 sts. (90 sts)

Row 5: 1dc in each st to end. (90 sts)
Change to B.

Rows 6–7: 1dc in each st. (90 sts)
Change to A.

Rows 8–9: 1dc in each st. (90 sts)
Change to B.

Row 10: 3ch, *1Cl in next st, miss 1 st; rep from * to last st, 1htr.
Change to A.

Rows 11–12: 2ch, 1htr in each st to end.

Row 13: 2ch, *1htr in each of next 7 sts, htr2tog; rep from * to end. (80 sts)
Change to B.

Row 14: 3ch, miss first st, *1Cl in next st, miss 1 st; rep from * to last st, 1htr.
Change to A.

Row 15: 1ch, 1dc in each st to end.

Row 16: 2ch, *1htr in each of next 6 sts, htr2tog; rep from * to end. (70 sts)

Row 17: 2ch, *1htr in each st to end.

Row 18: 2ch, *1htr in each of next 5 sts, htr2tog; rep from * to end. (60 sts)

Row 19: 2ch, *1htr in each st to end.

Row 20: 2ch, *1htr in each of next 4 sts, htr2tog; rep from * to end. (50 sts)

Row 21: Rep Row 19.

Row 22: 2ch, htr2tog, *1htr in each of next 3 sts, htr2tog; rep from * to end. (40 sts)

Row 23: 2ch, *1htr in each of next 2 sts, htr2tog; rep from * to end. (30 sts)

Row 24: 2ch, *htr2tog, 1htr in next st; rep from * to end. (20 sts)
    Fasten off leaving a long tail approx 30cm (12in).

Finishing

Sew in ends.

    Make a running stitch around last row. Pull yarn tight and gather top together, then sew in securely.

    Oversew seam together.

    Using A and B together, wrap the yarn around two or three fingers approx 80 times. Gently slide the yarn off your fingers and tie a knot in the centre very securely. The pompom will now have loops on either side of the knot. Cut all the loops; trim and fluff the pompom into shape and sew onto top of hat.

Flower Bonnet

This little bonnet has a really vintage look with different pinks, purples and yellow flowers sewn onto a basic bonnet shape and tied with a pretty ribbon under the chin. It's a lovely warm, cosy hat for those chilly days walking in the park.

EXPERT ADVICE

Make enough flowers to fit all around the hat and completely cover the surface of the base bonnet. Always sew in ends and weave in and out of stitches at back of centres to close the holes.

Materials

Rooster Almerino Baby

→ 1 x 50g (1¾oz) ball – approx 125m (136yds) – of shade 502 Seashell (off white) (A)

→ Scraps of shade 503 Sandcastle (yellow), 502 Seashell (off white), 507 Urchin (light pink), 506 Bikini (dark pink), 511 Anemone (purple), 504 Seaweed (green), 512 Horizon (lilac)

→ 3mm (D/3) crochet hook

→ 1m (40in) of 1.5cm (⅝in) wide ribbon

Abbreviations

ch chain; **dc** double crochet; **dtr** double treble; **htr** half treble; **rep** repeat; **sp** space; **ss** slip stitch; **st(s)** stitch(es); **tr** treble; **trtr** triple treble

Size

To fit age: 0–6 months

Finished size

Circumference: approx 37.5cm (15in)

Tension

15 sts x 8 rows over a 10cm (4in) square working treble using a 3mm (D/3) hook.

Bonnet

Using A, make 4ch, ss in first ch to form a ring.

Round 1: 2ch (counts as 1htr), 15htr in ring, join with ss in top of first 2-ch. (16 sts)

Round 2: 3ch, 1tr in next st, 2tr in next and each st to end, join with a ss in top of first 3-ch. (32 sts)

Round 3: 3ch, 1tr in base of first 3-ch, *1tr in each of next 2 sts, 2tr in next st; rep from * around, join with ss in top of first 3-ch. (42 sts)

Round 4: 3ch, 1tr in base of first 3-ch, *1tr in each of next 3 sts, 2tr in next st; rep from * around, join with ss in top of first 3-ch. (52 sts)

Round 5: 3ch, 1tr in base of first 3-ch, 1tr in each st around, join with ss in top of first 3-ch. (52 sts)

Round 6: 1ch, 1dc in between each tr to end, join with ss in top of first 1-ch. (52 sts)

Rep Rounds 5 and 6 three times more.

Round 13: Rep Round 5.

Round 14: 1ch, *miss 1 st, 1dc in next st, miss 1 st, 5tr in next st (1 shell); rep from * until 8 shells are made ending 1dc, 1ss in next st.

Fasten off.

Lazy daisy (make approx 7)

Using first colour, make 6ch, ss in first ch to form a ring.

Round 1: 1ch, 11dc in ring, join in next colour, ss to join in first 1-ch. (12 sts)

Petals:

Continue with second colour.

Round 2: [9ch, ss in next st] 12 times, ending with ss in ss of first round.

Weave around centre to close centre hole.
Fasten off.

Apple blossom (make approx 4)

Using first colour, make 4ch, ss in first ch to form a ring.

Round 1: 2ch, 9dc in ring, using second colour, ss in top of first 2-ch.

Continue with second colour.

Round 2: 1ch *[1dtr, 2trtr, 1dtr] in next st, ss in next st; rep from * 3 times more. [1dtr, 2trtr, 1dtr] in next st, ss in first 1-ch. (5 petals)

Fasten off.

Petal blossom (make approx 10)

Using any colour, make 6ch, ss in first ch to form a ring.

16dc in ring, join with ss, *3ch, 1tr in each of next 2 sts, 3ch, ss in next st; rep from * 4 more times. (5 petals)

Weave around centre to close centre hole.
Fasten off.

Remember me blossom (make approx 5)

Using first colour, make 4ch, ss in first ch to form a ring.

Round 1: 2ch, 9dc in ring, using second colour, ss in top of first 2-ch. (10 sts)

Continue with second colour.

Round 2: 5ch, 1trtr in each of next 9 sts, ss in top of first 5-ch.

Fasten off.
Turn petals inside out.

Cherry blossom (make approx 5)

Using any colour, make 4ch, ss in first ch to form a ring.

*3ch, 1tr in ring, 3ch, ss in ring; rep from * until 5 petals are made.

Fasten off.

Finishing

Use a tapestry needle to weave loose ends around centre of flowers to close centre hole. Stitch flowers to bonnet. Sew in ends.

Cut ribbon in half and attach each end approx 1cm (½in) down from last shell edge.

Star Stitch Bootees

Use a pretty toggle to embellish these cute little bootees, which match the Toggle Jacket on page 92. The star stitch is simple once you get the idea and these would make a perfect gift.

Materials

Rooster Almerino Baby
➜ 1 x 50g (1¾oz) ball – approx 125m (136yds) – of shade 504 Seaweed (green)
➜ 3mm (D/3) crochet hook
➜ 2 small toggle buttons

Abbreviations

ch chain; **dc** double crochet; **htr** half treble; **patt** pattern; **rep** repeat; **RS** right side; **ss** slip stitch; **st(s)** stitch(es); **yrh** yarn round hook

Special abbreviations

SS1 (Star Stitch 1) 3ch, insert hook in second ch from hook, yrh, pull yarn through (2 loops on hook), insert hook in next ch, yrh, pull yarn through (3 loops on hook), insert hook in base of ch, yrh, pull yarn through (4 loops on hook), insert hook in each of next 2 sts bringing a loop through each time (6 loops on the hook) yrh, pull yarn through all 6 loops, 1ch

SS2 (Star Stitch 2) insert hook through 1-ch of SS just made, pull yarn through (2 loops), insert hook through front of last loop of previous SS, pull yarn through, insert hook through base st of last loop of previous SS, pull yarn through, *insert hook through next st and pull loop through; rep from * once more (6 loops on hook), yrh, pull yarn through all 6 loops, 1ch.

Base (make 2)

Make 14ch.

Round 1: 2dc in second ch from hook, 1dc in each of next 5ch, 1htr in each of next 5ch, 2htr in next ch, 3htr in last ch. (17 sts)
Working on other side of chain, 2htr in next ch, 1htr in each of next 5ch, 1dc in each of next 5 sts, 2dc in last ch, join with ss in top of first dc. (31 sts)

Round 2: 3ch, 2tr in base of ss, 1tr in next st, 2tr in next st. 1tr in each of next 9 sts, *3tr in next st, 1tr in next st; rep from * three times more, 1tr in each of next 9 sts, 2tr in next st, join with ss in top of first 3-ch. (41 sts)

Round 3: 3ch, 1tr in base of ss, 1tr in each of next 20 sts, 2tr in next st, 1tr in next st, 2tr in next st, 1tr in each of next 17 sts, 2tr in

Size

To fit age: 0–6 months

Finished size

Length: approx 9cm (3½in)

next st, join with ss in top of first 3-ch.
(46 sts)

Begin working star st patt in rows:

Row 1: [SS1 (once only), SS2] to end of row, join with ss in first 3-ch, turn.

Row 2: 2ch, 2htr in centre of each star stitch to end of row, join with ss in top of first 3-ch. (46 sts)

Fasten off.

Top (make 1 left and 1 right)

Make 40ch.

Row 1: SS1 to end of row.

Row 2: 2ch, 2htr in centre of each star stitch to end of row, join with ss in top of first 3-ch.

Row 3: SS1 once, SS2 to end of row, join with a ss in first 2-ch.

Row 4: As Row 2.(For left foot shaping only, fasten off and see instruction below for left foot shaping).

Shaping for right foot:

Row 1: SS1 once, [SS2] four times, 1htr in top of 2-ch from previous row, turn.

Row 2: 2ch, 1htr in centre of first star stitch, *2htr in centre of each of next 2 star stitches, 1htr in last star stitch, 1dc in top of first star stitch from previous row, turn.

Row 3: SS1 once, [SS2] three times, 1htr in top of 2-ch from previous row, turn.

Row 4: 2ch, 1htr in centre of first star stitch, 2htr in next star stitch, 1htr into last star stitch, 1dc in top of star stitch from previous row, turn.

Row 5: SS1 once, SS2 once, 1htr in top of 2-ch from previous row, turn.

Fasten off.

Shaping for left foot:

Count 11 sts from left-hand side of work and join yarn in eleventh stitch. Repeat Rows 1–5 as for right foot shaping.

Fasten off.

Finishing

With RS facing, match centre top with centre base and pin. To create flap for toggle, start sewing from two star stitches down and then sew top around bootee.

Sew toggle button onto side back.

Toggle loop:

Pick up 1 st at front side corresponding with toggle, make 8ch, join with a ss in first ch.

Fasten off.

Sew in ends.

Flower Cot Blanket

A warm cosy blanket, big enough for a cot. This is made up of squares, so a great project and easy to make one or two squares per evening before the baby is born.

Materials

Rooster Almerino Aran

➜ 10 x 50g (1¾oz) balls – approx 940m (1030yds) – of shade 301 Cornish (off white) (A)

➜ 6 x 50g (1¾oz) balls – approx 564m (618yds) – of shade 303 Strawberry Cream (pale pink) (B)

➜ 4.5mm (G/6) and 5mm (H/8) crochet hook

Abbreviations

beg beginning; **ch** chain; **dc** double crochet; **htr** half treble; **patt** pattern; **rep** repeat; **sp(s)** space(es); **ss** slip stitch; **st(s)** stitch(es); **yrh** yarn round hook

Finished size

Approx 70 x 95cm (28 x 38in)

Tension

Each square measures approx 12.5 x 12.5cm (5 x 5in).

Flower square (make 35)

Using A and 4.5mm (G/6) hook, make 8ch, join with ss in first ch to make a ring.

Round 1: 1ch, 18dc into ring, ss in first dc. (18 sts)

Round 2: 1ch, *3ch, miss 2 sts, 1dc in next st; rep from * 5 times more, ss in first of 3-ch. (6 loops)

Round 3: 1ch, [1dc, 3ch, 5tr, 3ch, 1dc] into each of next 6 ch sps, ss in first 1-ch. (6 petals)

Round 4: 1ch, [1dc between 2-dc from previous round (between two petals), 5ch behind petal of previous round] 6 times, ss in first ch. (6 petals)

Round 5: 1ch, [1dc, 3ch, 7tr, 3ch, 1dc] in each of next 6 5-ch sps, ss in first ch.

Fasten off.

Round 6: Join B between 2-dc of previous round (between any two petals), 1ch, 1dc into same sp, [6ch (working behind petals) 1dc between next 2-dc of previous round] 6 times, ss in first ch.

Round 7: Ss in next sp, 3ch (counts as 1tr), *[4tr, 2ch, 2tr] into same sp, 6tr in next sp, [2tr, 2ch, 4tr] in next sp**, 1tr in next sp; rep from * to ** once more, ss in top of first 3-ch.

Round 8: 3ch (counts as 1tr), 1tr in each of next 4-tr from previous round, *[3tr, 2ch, 3tr] in next 2-ch sp, 1tr in each of next 9-tr; rep from * to last 4tr, 1tr in each of last 4-tr, join with a ss into top of first 3-ch.

Round 9: 3ch, *1tr in each st to next corner sp, [3tr, 2ch, 3tr] into corner sp; rep from * to end, ss into top of first 3-ch.

Fasten off.

Finishing

Sew in ends. Arrange squares 7 down by 5 across.

Using A, work a dc seam to join squares together.

Edging:

With RS facing and using 5mm (H/8) hook, join A in any corner ch sp.

Round 1: 1ch, 1dc in same ch sp (first corner), *1dc in each st along each square to next corner, (do not make a dc into the seams, but make 1dc each side of each seam), 2dc in corner ch sp; rep from * twice more, 1dc in each st to last corner, join with ss in first 1-ch.

Round 2: 3ch, 2tr in same sp as 3-ch (first corner), *1tr in each st to next corner, 3tr in corner st; rep from * twice more, 1tr in each st to last corner, join with ss in top of first 3-ch. Break off A.

Round 3: Join in B, *1dc in next st, miss next st, 5tr in next st, miss next st; rep from * to end, join with ss into joining st.

Fasten off.

CHAPTER THREE

Jackets, Shawls and Dresses

Hooded Jacket

A very cool and trendy jacket. It's embellished with a double row of big colourful buttons at the front and a bright orange pompom at the point on the hood. So cute, everyone in the family will want one!

Materials

Rooster Almerino Aran

➜ 5:5:6:6:7:7 x 50g (1¾oz) balls – approx 470:470:564:564:658:658m (515:515:618:618:721:721yds) – of shade 315 Shimmer (pale grey) (A)

➜ 1 x 50g (1¾oz) ball – approx 94m (103yds) – of shade 318 Coral (orange) (B)

➜ 4mm (F/5) crochet hook

➜ 6 x 2.5cm (1in) diameter 4-hole buttons in a variety of colours

Abbreviations

ch chain; **cont** continue; **dc** double crochet; **patt** pattern(s); **rep** repeat; **RS** right side; **ss** slip stitch; **st(s)** stitch(es); **WS** wrong side

Special abbreviation

V-st 1dc, 1ch, 1dc in next st.

Size

To fit age: 0–3:3–6:6–12:12–18:18–24:24–36 months

Finished size

Chest	(cm):	48	54	60	67.5	72	80
	(in):	19¼	21½	24	27	29	32
Length	(cm):	22.5	26.5	31	35	39	42
	(in):	9	10½	12¼	14	15½	17
Sleeve seam	(cm):	12.5	15.5	19.5	26	27.5	30
	(in):	5	6¼	7¾	10¼	11	12

Tension

8 patt x 18 rows over a 10cm (4in) square using a 4mm (F/5) hook.

Body

Using A, make 102:**114**:126:**138**:150:**162** ch.

Row 1: 1dc in second ch from hook, miss 1 ch, *1V-st in next ch, miss 2 ch; rep from * to end, ending last rep miss 1 ch, 1dc in last ch, turn. (101:**113**:125:**137**:149:**161** sts)

Row 2 (patt row): 1ch, 1dc in first dc, miss 2 sts, *make 1V-st in next st, miss 2 sts; rep from * to end, ending last rep miss 1 dc, 1dc in last st.

Rep Row 2 until body measures 12:**13**:15:**17.5**:19:**21**cm (4¾:**5¼**:6:**7**:7½:**8½**in) ending with a RS row.

First buttonhole:

Next row: With WS facing, 1ch, 1dc in first dc, 3ch, miss 1 V-st group, *1V-st in next ch sp; rep from * ending miss 1 dc, 1dc in last st. (101:**113**:125:**137**:149:**161** sts, 33:**37**:41:**45**:49:**53** patts)

Next row: Patt to buttonhole space, 1V-st in buttonhole sp, patt to end.

Work 6 rows in patt.

Divide for armholes:

Work 7:**8**:9:**10**:11:**12** patt, miss 1 dc, 1dc in next dc, turn.

Working on following 23:**26**:29:**32**:35:**38** sts only, work 7:**8**:9:**10**:11:**12** patt for left front.

Work 4 rows in patt.

Next two rows: Rep two buttonhole rows as before.

Continue working straight for 10 rows.

Next two rows: Rep two buttonhole rows as before.

Continue working straight until armhole measures 12:**12**:12.5:**14**:15:**17.5**cm (4¾:**4¾**:5:**5½**:6:**7**in) ending with a WS row.

Work 1 more row in patt.

Fasten off.

Shoulder:

Place a marker 9:**11**:13:**15**:17:**19** sts in from armhole edge to mark inner edge of shoulder seam leaving 14:**15**:16:**17**:18:**19** sts unworked at front opening edge.

Shape back:

With WS facing, return to last complete row worked, miss next 10 sts, join yarn in next dc, 1ch, 1dc in joining st, miss 1 dc, 1V-st in next ch sp, patt until 11:**13**:15:**17**:19:**21** patt in total have been worked, miss 1 dc, 1dc in next dc, turn.

Work on these 35:**41**:47:**53**:59:**65** sts, 11:**13**:15:**17**:19:**21** patt (back) until work measures 10.5:**12.5**:14:**15**:16.5:**17.5**cm (4¼:**5**:5½:**6**:6½:**7**in) ending with a RS row.

Fasten off.

Shoulder:

Place marker either side of centre 17:**19**:21:**23**:25:**27** sts for back neck.

Shape right front:

With WS facing, return to last complete row worked, miss next 10 sts, join yarn in next dc, 1ch, 1dc in joining st, 1ch, miss 1 dc, 1V-st in next ch sp, patt to end, turn.
(23:**26**:29:**32**:35:**38** sts, 7:**8**:9:**10**:11:**12** patt)

Finish to match left front.

Do not fasten off at end of right front, place loop onto safety pin (to be used later for hood).

Sleeves (make 2)

Make 24:**27**:27:**30**:30:**33**ch.

Rep Rows 1 and 2 as for Body.
(23:**26**:26:**29**:29:**32** sts, 7:**8**:8:**9**:9:**10** patt)

Row 3: 1ch, 2dc in first dc, miss 1 dc, 1V-st in next ch sp, patt until V-st has been worked in last ch sp, miss 1 dc, 2dc in first dc, turn.

Row 4: 1ch, 2dc in first dc, 1dc in next dc, miss 1 dc, 1 V-st in next ch sp, patt until V-st has been worked in last ch sp, miss 1 dc, 1dc in next dc, 2dc in last dc, turn.

Row 5: 1ch, 1dc in first dc, 1V-st in next dc, miss 2 dc, 1V-st in next ch sp, patt until V-st has been worked in last ch sp, miss 2 dc, 1V-st in next dc, 1dc in last dc, turn.
(29:**32**:32:**35**:35:**37** sts, 9:**10**:10:**11**:11:**12** patt)

Work 1:**3**:3:**5**:5:**6** rows in patt.

Rep last 4:**6**:6:**8**:8:**9** rows 1:**1**:2:**2**:3:**4** times more, then Rows 3–5 once again.
(41:**44**:50:**53**:56:**62** sts, 13:**14**:16:**17**:18:**20** patt)

Work straight in patt until sleeve measures 12.5:**15.5**:19.5:**26**:27.5:**30**cm (5:**6¼**:7¾:**10¼**:11:**12**in).

Shape top:

Place markers at each end of last row to mark top of sleeve seam.

Work a further 3 rows.

Fasten off.

Finishing

Join shoulder seams.

Hood:

Pick up loop left on safety pin at end of right front. Work across sts of right front neck, back neck, left front neck as follows:

1ch, 1dc in first dc, miss 1 dc, 1V-st in next ch sp, miss 2 dc, 1V-st in next ch sp, [miss 1 st, 1V-st in next st] 8:**9**:10:**11**:12:**13** times, 1V-st in next ch sp (centre back neck ch sp), [1V-st in next st, miss 1 st] 8:**9**:10:**11**:12:**13** times, 1V-st in next ch sp, miss 2 dc, 1V-st in next ch sp, miss 1 dc, 1dc in last dc, turn.
(65:**71**:77:**83**:89:**95** sts, 21:**23**:25:**27**:29:**31** patt)

Work in patt until hood measures 17.5:**19**:20.5:**22**:21.5:**25**cm (7:**7½**:8¼:**8½**:9:**10**in).

Fold hood in half with RS together and join using overstitch with yarn sewing needle.

Fasten off.

Join sleeve seams below markers. Match sleeve markers to centre of sts missed at underarm and centre of last row of sleeve to shoulder seam, sew sleeves into armholes.

Using B make a small pompom and sew onto tip of hood.

Buttonband and edging

With RS facing miss corner st at right front bottom edge and join yarn in next st up side.

Row 1: Dc evenly along right front, hood, left front, bottom edge, making 3dc in corner st of bottom left front, ending 3dc in corner st at bottom right front. Join with ss in first dc.

Row 2: 1ch, 1dc in each st up right front edge finishing at start of hood, turn.

Rows 3–4: 1ch, 1dc in each st to end.

Row 5: 1ch, 1dc in each st to end, make 2dc in next st around corner. Join with ss in first 3-dc from Row 1.

Fasten off.

Poncho

Ponchos are ideal for slipping on for extra warmth on chilly spring or autumn days. This toddler poncho is made using simple clusters and embellished with a pretty flower.

Materials

Rooster Almerino DK

→ 4 x 50g (1¾oz) balls – approx 450m (496yds) – of shade 211 Brighton Rock (bright pink) (A)

→ Small amounts of shade 201 Cornish (off white) (B) and 216 Pier (pale green) (C)

→ 4mm (F/5) crochet hook

Abbreviations

ch chain; **ch sp** chain space; **dc** double crochet; **htr** half treble; **patt** pattern; **rep** repeat; **sp** space; **ss** slip stitch; **st(s)** stitch(es); **WS** wrong side; **yrh** yarn round hook

Special abbreviations

Cl (Cluster) yrh, insert hook in st, yrh, pull yarn through, yrh, insert hook in same st, yrh, pull yarn through, yrh, insert hook in same st, yrh, pull yarn through, yrh (7 loops on hook), pull yarn through all 7 loops on hook, yrh, 1ch

make corner 1Cl, 3ch, 1Cl

Size

To fit age: 6–18 months.

Finished size

Circumference: 50cm (20in)

Length: 30cm (12in)

Tension

8 clusters x 6½ rows over a 10cm (4in) square using a 4mm (F/5) crochet hook.

Poncho

Using A, make 76ch, join with ss in first ch, taking care not to twist chain.

Round 1: 1Cl, miss 1 ch, *1Cl, miss 1 ch; rep from * to end, ss to top of first Cl. (38 clusters)

Round 2: 1Cl in first ch sp, [1Cl in next ch sp] 17 times (18 clusters), make corner in next ch sp, 1Cl, 3ch, 1Cl, 18Cl in the last ch sp, make corner, 1Cl, 3ch, 1Cl, ss to top of first Cl. (36 clusters + 2 corners)

Round 3: 1Cl in sp below in same ss from end of previous row, [1Cl in each ch sp] 18 times (19 clusters), make corner in 3-ch sp, [1Cl in each following ch sp] 19 times, make corner in 3-ch sp, ss to top of first Cl. (38 clusters + 2 corners)

Round 4: 1Cl in sp below finishing ss, [1Cl in each ch sp] 19 times (20 clusters), make corner in 3-ch sp, [1Cl in each ch sp] 20 times, make corner in 3-ch sp, ss to top of first Cl. (40 clusters + 2 corners)

Round 5: 1Cl in sp below finishing ss, [1Cl in each ch sp] 20 times (21 clusters), make corner in 3-ch sp, [1Cl in each ch sp] 21 times, make corner in 3-ch sp, ss to top of first Cl. (42 clusters + 2 corners)

Round 6: 1Cl in sp below finishing ss, [1Cl in each ch sp] 21 times (22 clusters), make corner in 3-ch sp, [1Cl in each ch sp] 22 times, make corner in 3-ch sp, ss to top of first Cl. (44 clusters + 2 corners)

Round 7: 1Cl in sp below finishing ss, [1Cl in each ch sp] 22 times (23 clusters), make corner in 3-ch sp, [1Cl in each ch sp] 23 times, make corner in 3-ch sp, ss to top of first Cl. (46 clusters + 2 corners)

Round 8: 1Cl in sp below finishing ss, [1Cl in each ch sp] 23 times (24 clusters), make corner in 3-ch sp, [1Cl in each ch sp] 24 times,

make corner in 3-ch sp, ss to top of first Cl. (48 clusters + 2 corners)

Round 9: 1Cl in sp below finishing ss, [1Cl in each ch sp] 24 times (25 clusters), make corner in 3-ch sp, [1Cl in each ch sp] 25 times, make corner in 3-ch sp, ss to top of first Cl. (50 clusters + 2 corners)

Round 10: 1Cl in sp below finishing ss, [1Cl in each ch sp] 25 times (26 clusters), make corner in 3-ch sp, [1Cl in each ch sp] 26 times, make corner in 3-ch sp, ss to top of first Cl. (52 clusters + 2 corners)

Round 11: 1Cl in sp below finishing ss, [1Cl in each ch sp] 26 times (27 clusters), make corner in 3-ch sp, [1Cl in each ch sp] 27 times, make corner in 3-ch sp, ss to top of first Cl. (54 clusters + 2 corners)

Round 12: 1Cl in sp below finishing ss, [1Cl in each ch sp] 27 times (28 clusters), make corner in 3-ch sp, [1Cl in each ch sp] 28 times, make corner in 3-ch sp, ss to top of first Cl. (56 clusters + 2 corners)

Round 13: 1Cl in sp below finishing ss, [1Cl in each ch sp] 28 times (29 clusters), make corner in 3-ch sp, [1Cl in each ch sp] 29 times, make corner in 3-ch sp, ss to top of first Cl. (58 clusters + 2 corners)

Round 14: 1Cl in sp below finishing ss, [1Cl in each ch sp] 29 times (30 clusters), make corner in 3-ch sp, [1Cl in each ch sp] 30 times, make corner in 3-ch sp, ss to top of first Cl. (60 clusters + 2 corners)

Round 15: 1Cl in sp below finishing ss, [1Cl in each ch sp] 30 times (31 clusters), make corner in 3-ch sp, [1Cl in each ch sp] 31 times, make corner in 3-ch sp, ss to top of first Cl. (62 clusters + 2 corners)

Round 16: 1Cl in sp below finishing ss, [1Cl in each ch sp] 31 times (32 clusters), make corner in 3-ch sp, [1Cl in each ch sp] 32 times, make corner in 3-ch sp, ss to top of first Cl. (64 clusters + 2 corners)

Round 17: 1Cl in sp below finishing ss, [1Cl in each ch sp] 32 times (33 clusters), make corner in 3-ch sp, [1Cl in each ch sp] 33 times, make corner in 3-ch sp, ss to top of first Cl. (66 clusters + 2 corners)

Round 18: 1Cl in sp below finishing ss, [1Cl in each ch sp] 33 times (34 clusters), make corner in 3-ch sp, [1Cl in each ch sp] 34 times, make corner in 3-ch sp, ss to top of first Cl. (68 clusters + 2 corners)

Round 19: 1Cl in sp below finishing ss, [1Cl in each ch sp] 34 times (35 clusters), make corner in 3-ch sp, [1Cl in each ch sp] 35 times, make corner in 3-ch sp, ss to top of first Cl. (70 clusters + 2 corners)

Round 20: 1Cl in sp below finishing ss, [1Cl in each ch sp] 35 times (36 clusters), make corner in 3-ch sp, [1Cl in each ch sp] 36 times, make corner in 3-ch sp, ss to top of first Cl. (72 clusters + 2 corners)

Round 21: 1Cl in sp below finishing ss, [1Cl in each ch sp] 36 times (37 clusters), make corner in 3-ch sp, [1Cl in each ch sp] 37 times, make corner in 3-ch sp, ss to top of first Cl. (74 clusters + 2 corners)

Round 22: 1Cl in sp below finishing ss, [1Cl in each ch sp] 37 times (38 clusters), make corner in 3-ch sp, [1Cl in each ch sp] 38 times, make corner in 3-ch sp, ss to top of first Cl. (76 clusters + 2 corners)

Round 23: 1Cl in sp below finishing ss, [1Cl in each ch sp] 38 times (39 clusters), make corner in 3-ch sp, [1Cl in each ch sp] 39 times, make corner in 3-ch sp, ss to top of first Cl. (78 clusters + 2 corners)

Round 24: 1Cl in sp below finishing ss, [1Cl in each ch sp] 39 times (40 clusters), make corner in 3-ch sp, [1Cl in each ch sp] 40 times, make corner in 3-ch sp, ss to top of first Cl. (80 clusters + 2 corners)

Do not fasten off.

Bottom edging:

1ch, 1dc in same space as chain (between 2-clusters of previous round), 1dc in each st and ch sp to end, ss to top of first dc.

Fasten off.

Neck edging:

Join yarn to ch at centre back neck edge.

Round 1: 1dc in each st and ch sp to end, ss in first dc.

Rep Round 1 twice more.

Fasten off.

Large flower

Using B, make 5ch, join with a ss in first ch to make a ring.

Round 1: *1dc, 1tr, 1dc in ring; rep from * 3 times. (4 petals)

Round 2: *2ch, from WS ss in base of second dc of next petal (pick up 2 loops); rep from * 3 times more, slip last st in first ss. (4 loops)

Round 3: *4tr in next 2ch sp (at back), ss in same ch sp; rep from * 3 times more.

Fasten off.

Change to C, join yarn at base of highest point of previous round.

Round 4: *3ch, ss in middle of base of next petal (pick up 2 loops); rep from * 3 times more, slip last st in joining st.

Round 5: *8tr in next 3-ch sp, ss in same 3-ch sp; rep from * 3 times more, slip last st in joining st.

Fasten off.

Small flower (make 2)

Using B, make 5ch, join with a ss in first ch to make a ring.

Round 1: *1dc, 1tr, 1dc in ring, rep from * 3 times. (4 petals)

Round 2: *2ch, from WS ss in base of second dc of next petal (pick up 2 loops); rep from * 3 times more, slip last st in first ss. (4 loops)

Join in C.

Round 3: *4tr in next 2ch sp (at back), ss in same ch sp; rep from * 3 times more.

Fasten off.

Joining plait

Cut six 60cm (24in) lengths of A and tie in the middle. Taking each side separately, plait the strands until there is approx 4cm (1½in) of yarn left at the bottom. Secure the plait with a length of yarn.

Finishing

Sew in ends.

Position the plait in the centre of the reverse of the large flower and secure. Sew a small flower on each end of the plait at the point where you secured each side. Position the large flower on the shoulder of the poncho and sew on.

Tasselled Baby Poncho

This is a really popular and classic poncho, one of the first crochet projects I ever made. It is an excellent gift or quick project for a baby – you can finish it in one evening!

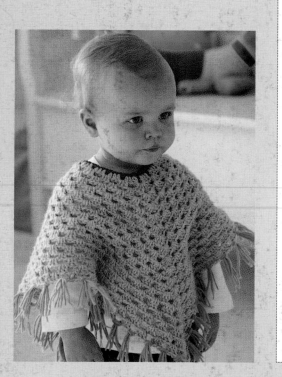

Materials

Rooster Almerino DK

→ 1:**1** x 50g (1¾oz) ball – approx 112.5:**112.5**m (124:**124**yds) – of shade 207 Gooseberry (green) (A)
→ 2:**3** x 50g (1¾oz) balls – approx 225:**337.5**m (248:**372**yds) – of shade 219 Sandcastle (yellow) (B)
→ 1:**1** x 50g (1¾oz) ball – approx 112.5:**112.5**m (124:**124**yds) – of shade 211 Brighton Rock (bright pink) (C)
→ 3.5mm (E/4) crochet hook

Abbreviations

ch chain; **dc** double crochet; **inc** increase; **patt** pattern(s); **rep** repeat; **sp** space; **ss** slip stitch; **st(s)** stitch(es); **tr** treble

Size

To fit age: 6–12:**12–18** months

Finished size

Length	(cm):	30	37.5
	(in):	12	15
Side length	(cm):	22.5	30
	(in):	9	12

Tension

5 patt x 9 rows over a 10cm (4in) square using a 3.5mm (E/4) hook.

Poncho

Using A, make 72:**88**ch, join with ss to form a ring.

Round 1: 1ch, 1dc in each ch to end, ss in first ch with B. (72:**88** sts)
Fasten off A.

Round 2: 3ch, 1tr in each of next 2 sts, 1ch, miss 1 st, *1tr in each of next 3 sts, 1ch, miss 1 st; rep from * to end, join with ss in top of first 3-ch.

Round 3: Ss in each of next 2 sts, ss in next ch sp, 3ch, [2tr, 1ch, 3tr] in same ch sp, *1ch, 3tr in next ch sp; rep from * 7:**9** times more, 1ch [3tr, 1ch, 3tr] in next ch sp, 1ch, 3tr in next ch sp; rep from * 7:**9** times more, 1ch, ss in top of first 3-tr.

Round 4: Ss in each of next 2 sts, ss in next ch sp, 3ch, [2tr, 1ch, 3tr] in same ch sp *1ch, 3tr in next ch sp; rep from * to next inc group from previous round, 1ch [3tr, 1ch, 3tr] in next ch sp (middle of inc group), 1ch, 3tr in next ch sp; rep from * to end of round, 1ch, ss in top of first 3-tr.

Rep Round 4 until 20:**26** rows in total have been worked (or make to required length).
Fasten off.

Finishing

Sew in ends.

Using C, make approx 5cm (2in) tassels by wrapping yarn around four fingers four times. Remove from fingers, cut yarn at bottom, insert top loop into space at bottom of poncho, pull other end through loop forming a tassel and trim.

Blossom Shawl

An heirloom project with a vintage feel. This shawl is made up from individual motifs and then decorated with little flowers around the edge to give it some movement.

Materials

Fyberspates Scrumptious 4-ply
→ 5 x 100g (3½oz) skeins – approx 1825m (1995yds) – of shade 303 Oyster (beige) (MC)
→ Small amount of various shades of pink (CC)
→ 3mm (D/3) crochet hook

Abbreviations

CC contrast colour; **ch** chain; **ch sp** chain space; **dc** double crochet; **htr** half treble; **MC** main colour; **rep** repeat; **sp** space; **ss** slip stitch; **st(s)** stitch(es); **tr** treble; **yrh** yarn round hook

Special abbreviations

3chpicot (3-chain picot) work 3ch, ss in third ch from hook, pull tight
trCl (treble cluster) *yrh, insert hook into ring, yrh, pull yarn through, yrh, pull yarn through 2 loops; rep from * twice more (4 loops on hook), yrh, pull yarn through all 4 loops (1tr cluster made)

Finished size

Approx 112 x 89cm (44 x 35in)

Main motif (make 86)

Using MC, make 8ch, join with ss in first ch to make a ring.

Round 1: 3ch, *yrh, insert hook through ring, yrh, pull yarn through, yrh, pull yarn through 2 loops (2 loops on hook); rep from * once more (3 loops on hook), yrh, draw yarn through all 3 loops, **5ch, 1trCl into ring; repeat from ** 10 times more. (12 clusters)

Round 2: 2ch, 1tr in the top of first trCl, 1ch, * make a 3chpicot, 5ch, 1dc in top of next trCl; rep from * 11 times more, ss in 1-ch at top of first trCl from previous round.

Round 3: Take yarn behind 3chpicot and ss in second ch of 5-ch arch, 3ch (counts as 1tr), 4tr in 5-ch sp, *5ch, [5tr in next 5-ch sp] twice; rep from * 4 times more, 5ch, 5tr in next 5-ch sp, ss into top of first 3-ch.

Round 4: Miss first st, dc in next st, 5tr in next 5-ch sp, 1ch, 3chpicot, 5tr in same 5-ch sp,

miss 2 sts, dc in next st, *7ch, miss 4 sts, 1dc in next st, 5tr in 5-ch sp, 1ch, 3chpicot, 5tr in same 5-ch sp, miss 2 sts, 1dc in next st, rep from * 4 times more, 7ch, miss 3 sts, ss in next st.

Fasten off.

Small flowers (make 28 in assorted shades)

Using CC, make 4ch, join with ss in first ch to make a ring.

6dc in ring.

*Ss in first dc, 3ch, 1tr in same st, 3ch, ss in same st; rep from * 5 times more. (6 petals)

Fasten off.

Finishing

Lay out a row of 10 main motifs, followed by a row of 9 main motifs; repeat this sequence three more times and finish with another row of 10 motifs.

Sew the main motifs together at the points and middle chain between points.

Position and stitch a flower on each point along the long edge of the shawl and in the middle of the centre motif of the curve on the short edge.

EXPERT ADVICE

Sew in the ends of each motif as you finish it.

Toggle Jacket

The pretty star stitch on this jacket makes it a really special piece of clothing. The wool is soft and really works well in this lovely colour.

Back

Make 58:**63**:69:**75**ch.

Row 1: 1dc in next ch from hook, 1dc in each ch to end. (56:**62**:68:**74** sts)

Row 2: SS1, SS2 to last st, 1htr in top of 3-ch from previous row. (27:**30**:33:**36** stars)

Row 3: 3ch, *2tr in centre of star; rep from * to end, 1htr in last st of last star of Row 2.

Rep Rows 2 and 3 until a total of 15:**15**:17:**19** rows have been worked.

Next row: Rep Row 2.

Back shaping for armhole:

Row 1: 3ch, miss first star stitch, *2tr in centre of next star; rep from * to last star, miss last star, 1htr in top of last st.

Row 2: SS1, SS2 to last st, 1htr in top of 3-ch from previous row. (25:**28**:31:**34** stars)

Rep Rows 1 and 2 another 3:**4**:5:**6** times more. (19:**20**:21:**22** stars)

Row 9: Rep Row 1.

Fasten off.

Left front

Make 33:**37**:39:**43**ch.

Row 1: 1dc in next ch from hook, 1dc in each ch to end. (32:**36**:38:**42** sts)

Row 2: SS1, SS2 to last st, 1htr in top of dc from previous row. (15:**17**:18:**20** stars)

Row 3: 3ch, *2tr in centre of star; rep from * to end, 1htr in last st of last star of Row 2.

Rep Rows 2 and 3 until a total of 15:**15**:17:**19** rows have been worked.

Next row: Rep Row 2.

Materials

Rooster Almerino Baby

➜ 3:**3**:4:**4** x 50g (1¾oz) balls – approx 375:**375**:500:**500**m (408:**408**:544:**544**yds) – of shade 504 Seaweed (green)

➜ 3.5mm (E/4) crochet hook

➜ 3 x wooden toggle buttons, each 2cm (¾in) long

Abbreviations

beg beginning; **ch** chain; **dc** double crochet; **dc2tog** (double crochet 2 together decrease) insert hook in next st, yrh, pull yarn through (2 loops on hook). Without finishing st, insert hook in next st, yrh, pull yarn through (3 loops on hook), yrh, pull yarn through all 3 loops on hook; **htr** half treble; **rep** repeat; **RS** right side; **ss** slip stitch; **st(s)** stitch(es); **tr** treble; **WS** wrong side; **yrh** yarn round hook

Special abbreviations

SS1 (Star Stitch 1) 3ch, insert hook in second ch from hook, pull yarn through, insert hook in third ch from hook, pull yarn through, insert hook in next st, pull loop through (4 loops on hook). Insert hook in next st, pull yarn through, insert hook in next st, pull yarn through (6 loops on hook), yrh, pull yarn through all 6 loops, 1ch

SS2 (Star Stitch 2) insert hook in base of ch just made, pull yarn through, insert hook in front of last st of previous star stitch, pull yarn through, insert hook in whole of same st, pull yarn through, insert hook in next st, pull yarn through, insert hook in next st, pull yarn through (6 loops), yrh, pull yarn through all 6 loops, 1ch

Size

To fit age: 3–6:**6–12**:12–18:**24–36** months

Finished size

Chest	**(cm)**:	52.5	**57.5**	62.5	**67.5**
	(in):	21	**23**	25	**27**
Length	**(cm)**:	25	**27.5**	30	**32.5**
	(in):	10	**11**	12	**13**
Sleeve seam	**(cm)**:	12.5	**17.5**	22.5	**27.5**
	(in):	5	**7**	9	**11**

Tension

11 stars x 5½ star patterns over a 10cm (4in) square using a 3.5mm (E/4) hook.

Shaping for left front armhole:

Row 1: With WS facing, 3ch *2tr in centre of next star from previous row; rep from * to last star, miss last star, 1htr in top of star of previous row.

Row 2: SS1, SS2 to end of row, 1htr in top of 3-ch from previous row. (14:**16**:17:**19** stars)

Rep last 2 rows 3:**4**:5:**6** times more.

Row 9: Rep Row 1.

Fasten off.

Right front

Make 33:**37**:39:**43**ch.

Row 1: 1dc in next ch from hook, 1dc in each ch to end. (32:**36**:38:**42** sts)

Row 2: SS1, SS2 to last st, 1htr in top of dc from previous row. (15:**17**:18:**20** stars)

Row 3: 3ch, miss 1 star, *2tr in centre of next star; rep from * to end, 1htr in top of last st of last star of Row 2.

Rep Rows 2 and 3 until a total of 15:**15**:17:**19** rows have been worked.

Next row: Rep Row 2.

Shaping for right front armhole:

Row 1: With WS facing, 3ch, miss 1 star, *2tr in centre of each star from previous row; rep from * to end, 1htr in last st of star of previous row.

Row 2: SS1, SS2 to end of row, 1htr in top of 3-ch from previous row. (14:**16**:17:**19** stars)

Rep last 2 rows 3:**4**:5:**6** times more.

Row 9: Rep Row 1.

Fasten off.

Sleeves (make 2)

Make 39:**41**:43:**45**ch.

Row 1: 1dc in next ch from hook, 1dc in each ch to end. (38:**40**:42:**44** sts)

Row 2: SS1, SS2 to end of row, 1htr in top of 3-ch from previous row. (18:**19**:20:**21** stars)

Row 3: 3ch, *2tr in centre of star from previous row; rep from * to last star, miss last star, 1htr in top of star of previous row.

Rep last 2 rows 5:**8**:10:**13** times more.

Next row: Rep Row 2.

Armhole shaping for sleeve:

Row 15: 3ch, miss one star stitch, *2tr in centre of next star; rep from * to last star stitch, miss last star stitch, 1htr in top of 3-ch from previous row.

Row 16: SS1, SS2 to end of row, 1htr in top of 3-ch from previous row. (16:**17**:18:**19** stars)

Rep last 2 rows 3:**4**:5:**6** times more.

(10:**9**:8:**7** stars)

Rep Row 15.

Fasten off.

Sew side and sleeve seams, fit sleeves.

Neck edging

With RS facing, join yarn at top of right front neck edge, 1dc in each of next 16:**18**:19:**21** sts (to beg of first sleeve top), [dc2tog, 1dc in each of next 4:**5**:5:**6** sts] three times, dc2tog, 1dc in each of next 4:**1**:2:**2** sts, [dc2tog, 1dc in each of next 5 sts] 3:**4**:4:**4** times, 1dc in each of next 2:**1**:1:**2** sts, [dc2tog, 1dc in each of next 4:**5**:5:**6** sts] three times, dc2tog, 1dc in each st across left front, turn.

Next row: 1ch, 1dc in each of next 16:**18**:19:**21** sts (front), dc2tog over next 16:**18**:20:**22** sts (sleeve), dc2tog, 1dc in each of next 20:**26**:27:**28** sts (back), dc2tog (back), dc2tog over next 16:**18**:20:**22** sts (second sleeve),

1dc in each of next 16:**18**:19:**21** sts (front). (70:**80**:87:**94** sts)

Do not fasten off.

Collar:

Row 1: 2ch, 1htr in each st. (70:**80**:87:**94** sts)

Row 2: 2ch, miss 1 st, 1htr in each of next 9:**10**:11:**13** sts, 2htr in next st, 1htr in each of next 10:**12**:13:**14** sts, 2htr in next st, 1htr in each of next 10:**12**:13:**14** sts, 2htr in next st, 1htr in each of next 10:**12**:13:**14** sts, 2htr in next st, 1htr in each of next 9:**10**:11:**13** sts, miss 1 st, 1htr in 2-ch from previous row.

Row 3: 2ch, miss 1 st, 1htr in each of next 9:**10**:11:**13** sts, 2htr in next st, 1htr in each of next 11:**12**:13:**14** sts, 2htr in next st, 1htr in each of next 11:**12**:13:**14** sts, 2htr in next st, 1htr in each of next 11:**12**:13:**14** sts, 2htr in next st, 1htr in each of next 9:**10**:12:**13** sts, miss 1 st, 1htr in 2-ch from previous row.

Row 4: 2ch, miss 1 st, 1htr in each st to last 2 sts, miss 1 st, 1htr in 2-ch from previous row.

Row 5: Rep Row 4.

Row 6: 2ch, miss 1 st, 1htr in each of next 5:**6**:7:**9** sts, 2htr in next st, 1htr in each of next 12:**13**:14:**15** sts, 2htr in next st, 1htr in each of next 12:**13**:14:**15** sts, 2htr in next st, 1htr in each of next 12:**13**:14:**15** sts, 2htr in next st, 1htr in each of next 12:**13**:14:**15** sts, 2htr in next st, 1htr in each of next 8:**9**:10:**12** sts, miss 1 st, 1htr in 2-ch from previous row.

Row 7: 1ch, miss 1 st, 1dc in each st to last 2 sts, miss 1 st, ss in 2-ch from previous row.

Fasten off.

Finishing

Sew in ends. Sew on toggle buttons.

Toggle loops (make one for each button):

Make 16ch. Fasten off.

Fold chain in half to make a loop and sew two ends onto jacket on opposite front edge to correspond with toggle buttons.

Petal Cape

A really sweet little cape made using an open shell stitch on the petals and a 'crocodile stitch' collar making scales or scallops around the neck.

Materials

Rooster Almerino Baby

➜ 3:4:5 x 50g (1¾oz) balls – approx 375:**500**:625m (408:**544**:680yds) – of shade 514 Lighthouse (red) (A)

Rooster Almerino DK

➜ 1 x 50g (1¾oz) ball – approx 112.5m (124yds) – of shade 203 Strawberry Cream (pale pink) (B)

➜ 3.5mm (E/4) crochet hook

Abbreviations

ch chain; **dc** double crochet; **patt** pattern; **rep** repeat; **RS** right side; **sp** space; **ss** slip stitch; **st(s)** stitch(es); **tr** treble; **yrh** yarn round hook

Size

To fit age: 3–12:**18–24**:24–36 months

Finished size

Circumference	(cm):	76.5	**86.5**	95
	(in):	30½	**34¼**	38
Length	(cm):	30	**35**	37
	(in):	12	**14**	14¾

Tension

3½ shell patterns x 8 rows over a 10cm (4in) square using a 3.5mm (E/4) hook.

Main body

Using A, make 91:**99**:107ch.

Row 1: 1tr in 3rd ch from hook, *1ch, miss 2 ch, [1tr, 3ch, 1tr] in next ch, 1ch, miss 2 ch, 1tr in each of next 3 ch; rep from * to end, omitting 1tr at end of last rep. (89:**97**:105 sts)

Row 2: 4ch (counts as 1tr, 1ch), 7tr in next 3-ch sp, *1ch, miss 2 tr, 1tr in next tr, 1ch, 7tr in next 3-ch sp; rep from * to last 3 tr, 1ch, miss 2 tr, 1tr in top of 3-ch.

Row 3: 4ch, 1tr in base of 4-ch, 1ch, miss 2 tr, 1tr in each of next 3 tr, *1ch, miss 2 tr, [1tr, 3ch, 1tr] in next tr, 1ch, miss 2 tr, 1tr in each of next 3 tr; rep from * to last 3 tr, miss 2 tr, [1tr, 1ch, 1tr] in third of 4-ch from previous row.

Row 4: 3ch (counts as 1tr), 3tr in first ch sp, 1ch, miss 2 tr, 1tr in next tr, *1ch, 7tr in next 3-ch sp, 1ch, miss 2 tr, 1tr in next tr; rep from * to last 3 tr, 1ch, miss 2 tr, 3tr in last ch sp, 1tr in third of 4-ch from previous row.

Row 5: 3ch, miss 1 tr, 1tr in next tr, *1ch, miss 2 tr, [1tr, 3ch, 1tr] in next tr, 1ch, miss 2 tr, 1tr in each of next 3 tr; rep from * to end, omitting

one tr at end of last rep and placing last tr in third of 3-ch from previous row.

Row 6: 4ch (counts as 1tr, 1ch), 9tr in next 3-ch sp, * 2ch, miss 3 tr, 1tr in next tr, 2ch, 9tr in next 3-ch sp; rep from * to last 3 tr, 2ch, miss 2 tr, 1tr in top of 3-ch.

Row 7: 4ch, 1tr in base of 4-ch, 2ch, miss 3 tr, 1tr in each of next 3 tr, * 2ch, miss 2 tr [1tr, 3ch, 1tr] in next tr, 2ch, miss 3 tr, 1tr in each of next 3 tr; rep from * to last 3 tr, 2ch, miss 3 tr, [1tr, 1ch, 1tr] in third of 4-ch.

Row 8: 3ch (counts as 1tr), 3tr in first ch sp, 2ch, miss 2 tr, 1tr in next tr, * 2ch, 9tr in next 3-ch sp, 2ch, miss 2 tr, 1tr in next tr; rep from * to last 3 tr, 2ch, miss 2 tr, 3tr in last ch sp, 1tr in third of 4-ch.

Row 9: 3ch, miss 1 tr, 1tr in next tr, 2ch, miss 2 tr, [1tr, 3ch, 1tr] in next tr, * 2ch, miss 3 tr, 1tr in each of next 3 tr, 2ch, miss 3 tr, [1tr, 3ch, 1tr] in next tr; rep from * to last 3 tr, make 2ch, miss 1 tr, 1tr in each of next 2 tr, 1tr in third of 4-ch.

Row 10: Rep Row 6.

Row 11: 4ch, 1tr in base of 4-ch, 2ch, miss 3 tr, 1tr in next tr, 2tr in next tr, 1tr in next tr, *2ch, miss 3 tr, [1tr, 3ch, 1tr] in next tr, 2ch, miss 3 tr, 1tr in next tr, 2tr in next tr, 1tr in next tr; rep from * to last 3 tr, 2ch, miss 3 tr, [1tr, 1ch, 1tr] in third of 4-ch from previous row.

Row 12: 3ch, 3tr in first ch sp, 2ch, miss 2 tr, 1tr in each of next 2 tr, miss 1 tr, * 2ch, 9tr in next 3-ch sp, 2ch, miss 1 tr, 1tr in each of next 2 tr, miss 1 tr; rep from * to last 2-ch sp, 2ch miss 2-ch sp, 3tr in last 4-ch sp, 1tr in top of 3-ch from previous row.

Row 13: 3ch, miss 1 tr, 1tr in next tr, 2ch, miss 2 tr, *1tr in next tr, 5ch, 1tr in next tr, 2ch, **miss 3 tr, 1tr in next tr, 2tr in next tr, 1tr in next tr, 2ch, miss 3 tr; rep from * to last rep, ending at **, miss 1 tr, 1tr in each of next 3 tr,

1tr in top of 3-ch from previous row.

Row 14: 5ch, 11tr in next 5-ch sp, * 3ch, miss 1 tr, 1tr in each of next 2 tr, miss 1 tr, 3ch, 11tr in next 5-ch sp; rep from * to last tr, 2ch, miss 1 tr, 1tr in top of 3-ch from previous row.

Row 15: 5ch, 1tr in base of 5-ch, *3ch, miss 4 tr, 1tr in next tr, 2tr in next tr, 1tr in next tr, miss 4 tr, 3ch, 1tr in next tr, 5ch, 1tr in next tr; rep from * to last 11 tr from previous row, miss 4 tr, 3ch, 1tr in next tr, 2tr in next tr, 1tr in next tr, miss 4 tr, 3ch, 1tr in 3rd of 5-ch from previous row.

Sizes 18–24:24–36 months only:

Row 16: 3ch, 4tr in first ch sp, 3ch, miss 1 tr, 1tr in each of next 2 tr, miss 1 tr, * 3ch, 11tr in next 5-ch sp, 3ch, miss 1 tr, 1tr in each of next 2 tr, miss 1 tr; rep from * to last 3-ch sp, 3ch miss 3-ch sp, 4tr in last 5-ch sp.

Row 17: 3ch, miss 1 tr, 1tr in next tr, 3ch, miss 2 tr, *1tr in next tr, 5ch, 1tr in next tr, 3ch, **miss 4 tr, 1tr in next tr, 2tr in next tr, 1tr in next tr, 3ch, miss 4 tr; rep from * to last rep, ending at **, miss 2 tr, 1tr in each of next 3 tr, 1tr in top of 3-ch from previous row.

Row 18: 5ch, 11tr in next 5-ch sp, * 3ch, miss 1 tr, 1tr in each of next 2 tr, miss 1 tr, 3ch, 11tr in next 5-ch sp; rep from * to last tr, 2ch, miss 1 tr, 1tr in top of 3-ch from previous row.

Row 19: 5ch, 1tr in base of 5-ch, * 3ch, miss 4 tr, 1tr in next tr, 2tr in next tr, 1tr in next tr, miss 4 tr, 3ch, 1tr in next tr, 5ch, 1tr in next tr; rep from * to last 11 tr from previous row, miss 4 tr, 3ch, 1tr in next tr, 2tr in next tr, 1tr in

next tr, miss 4 tr, 3ch, 1tr in third of 5-ch from previous row.

Do not fasten off.

Outer petals 1, 9 and 10:

Row 1 (RS facing): 7ch, 1dc in first tr, *3ch, miss 1 st, 1dc in next st; rep from * 7 times more, 4ch, miss 1 st, 1tr in next st, turn.

Row 2: 7ch, 1dc in next 3-ch sp, *3ch, 1dc in next ch sp; rep from * 6 times more, 4ch, 1tr in third ch of 7-ch from previous row.

Row 3: 7ch, 1dc in next 3-ch sp, *3ch, 1dc in next ch sp; rep from * 5 times more, 4ch, 1tr in third ch of 7-ch from previous row.

Row 4: 7ch, 1dc in next 3-ch sp, *3ch, 1dc in next ch sp; rep from * 4 times more, 4ch, 1tr in third ch of 7-ch from previous row.

Row 5: 7ch, 1dc in next 3-ch sp, *3ch, 1dc in next ch sp; rep from * 3 times more, 4ch, 1tr in third ch of 7-ch from previous row.

Row 6: 7ch, 1dc in next 3-ch sp, *3ch, 1dc in next ch sp; rep from * twice more, 4ch, 1tr in third ch of 7-ch from previous row.

Row 7: 7ch, 1dc in next 3-ch sp, *3ch, 1dc in next ch sp; rep from * once more, 4ch, 1tr in third ch of 7-ch from previous row.

Row 8: 7ch, 1dc in next 3-ch sp, 4ch, 1tr in third ch of 7-ch from previous row.

Row 9: 7ch, 1tr in dc, 4ch, 1tr in third ch of 7-ch from previous row.

Row 10: 3ch, 1dtr in tr, 3ch, ss in third ch of 5-ch from previous row.

Fasten off.

Inner petals 2–7:

Row 1: 5ch, 1tr in base of 5-ch, 4ch, miss 2 sts, 1dc in next st, *3ch, miss 1 st, 1dc in next st; rep from * 7 times more. 4ch, miss 2 sts, 1tr in each of next 2 sts, 5ch, turn.

Row 2: 1tr in base of 5-ch from previous row, 4ch, 1dc in next 3-ch sp, * 3ch, 1dc in next 3-ch sp; rep from * 6 times more. 4ch, 1tr in next tr, 1tr in third of 5-ch from previous row, 5ch, turn.

Row 3: 1tr in base of 5-ch from previous row, 4ch, 1dc in next 3-ch sp, * 3ch, 1dc in next 3-ch sp; rep from * 5 times more, 4ch, 1tr in next st, 1tr in third of 5-ch from previous row, 5ch, turn.

Continue as above having one 3-ch sp less on each row until one 3-ch sp remains, ending each row with 5ch.

Next row: 1tr in base of 5-ch, 4ch, 1dc in next 3-ch sp, 4ch, 1tr in next tr, 1tr in third of 5-ch from previous row.

Next row: 5ch, 1tr in base of first 5-ch, 3ch, 1tr in next dc, 3ch, 1tr in next tr, 1tr in third of 5-ch.

Next row: 5ch, 1tr in base of first 5-ch, 3ch, 1dtr in centre tr, 3ch, 1ss in third of 5-ch.

Fasten off.

With RS facing, join in same stitch as last ss from previous petal and rep Petal 2.

Petal 8:

With RS facing, join yarn in next st from ss from previous petal. Rep Petal 1.

Collar

Using A, make 82:**90**:98ch.

Row 1: 1dc in second ch from hook, 1dc in each ch to end. (81:**89**:97 sts)

Row 2: 3ch (counts as first tr), 1tr in base of first 3-ch, *2ch, miss next 2 sts, 1tr in each of next 2 sts; rep from * to end, 1ch. Do not turn.

Row 3: Yrh, insert hook in space between 2-tr group from previous row, from behind and from back of work to front, make 5tr in same space (if you turn work to the side, it's easier to make the stitch), 1ch, turn.

Yrh, insert hook from left to right (when row of dc is at bottom) and round back of second tr stalk, make 5tr around second tr stem. (1 scale made).

*Miss next 2-tr group, insert hook around first stalk of next tr group (back to front), work 5tr, 1ch, insert hook from left to right and round the stalk of second tr, make 5tr around stalk; rep from * to end of row, turn.

Row 4: 3ch, 1tr in base of 3-ch, *2ch. 2tr in the centre of scale from previous row, 2ch, 2tr in centre of 2-tr group from row 2; rep from * to end scale, 2ch, make 2tr in top edge of last scale, 1ch.

Row 5: Yrh, insert hook in space between 2-tr group from previous row, from behind and from back of work to front, make 5tr in same space (if you turn work to the side, it's easier to make the stitch), 1ch, turn.

Yrh, insert hook from left to right (when row of dc is at bottom) and round back of second tr stalk, make 5tr around second tr stalk. (1 scale made)

*Miss next 2-tr group, insert hook around first stalk of next tr group (back to front), work 5tr, 1ch, insert hook from left to right and round stalk of second tr, make 5tr around stalk; rep from * to end, make 1ss between last 2tr-group.

Row 6: 3ch, 1tr in base of 3-ch, *2ch. 2tr in centre of scale from previous row, 2ch, 2tr in centre of 2-tr group from 2 rows before; rep from * to end, ss in last centre of scale, 1ch, turn.

Row 7: Rep Row 3.

Size 24–36 months only:

Rep Rows 4–5 once more.

Fasten off.

Tie

Using A and yarn doubled, make a chain approx 76cm (30in) long.

Fasten off.

Finishing

Fit collar around neck edge and sew in place.

Thread tie on wrong side of collar by weaving in and out of tr groups. Using B, make two small pompoms (see page 71) and attach one on each end of tie.

Pink Baby Dress

Made in a light, soft yarn with a mix of alpaca and merino wool, this baby dress is easy to wear and embellished with a row of pretty flowers.

Materials

Rooster Almerino Baby

→ 4 x 50g (1¾oz) balls – approx 500m (544yds) – of shade 505 Candy Floss (pink) (A)

→ Scraps of shade 502 Seashell (off white) (B) and 504 Seaweed (green) (C)

→ 3mm (D/3) and 3.5mm (E/4) crochet hooks

→ 3 small buttons

Abbreviations

ch chain; **dc** double crochet; **rep** repeat; **RS** right side; **sp** space; **ss** slip stitch; **st(s)** stitch(es); **tr** treble

Size

To fit age: 6–9 months

Finished size

Chest: 55cm (22in)

Length: 36.5cm (14½in)

Tension

4 shells x 6 rows of pattern over a 10cm (4in) square using a 3.5mm (E/4) hook.

Yoke

Using A and 3.5mm (E/4) hook throughout, make 61ch.

Row 1: 1tr in fourth ch from hook, 1tr in each of next 57ch. (58 sts)

Row 2: 3ch, miss 1 st, 1tr in each of next 5 sts, *2tr in next st, 1tr in each of next 3 sts; rep from * 11 times more, 1tr in each of next 4 sts, 1tr in top of turning ch. (70 sts)

Row 3: 3ch, miss 1 st, 1tr in each of next 5 sts, *2tr in next st, 1tr in each of next 4 sts; rep from * 11 times more, 1tr in each of next 4 sts, 1tr in top of turning ch. (82 sts)

Row 4: 3ch, miss 1 st, 1tr in each of next 5 sts, *2tr in next st, 1tr in each of next 5 sts; rep from * 11 times more, 1tr in each of next 4 sts, 1tr in top of turning ch. (94 sts)

Row 5: 3ch, miss 1 st, 1tr in each of next 5 sts, *2tr in next st, 1tr in each of next 6 sts; rep from * 11 times more, 1tr in each of next 4 sts, 1tr in top of turning ch. (106 sts)

Row 6: 3ch, miss 1 st, 1tr in each of next 5 sts, *2tr in next st, 1tr in each of next 7 sts; rep from * 11 times more, 1tr in each of next 4 sts, 1tr in top of turning ch. (118 sts)

Row 7: 3ch, miss 1 st, 1tr in each of next 2 sts, 2tr in next st, 1tr in each of next 2 sts, 2tr in next st, *1tr in each of next 8 sts, 2tr in the next st; rep from * 4 times more. 1tr in each of next 3 sts, 2tr in next st, 1tr in each of next 4 sts, 2tr in next st, * 1tr in each of next 8 sts, 2tr in next st; rep from * 5 times more, 1tr in each of next 3 sts, 1tr in top of turning ch. (133 sts)

Do not fasten off.

Skirt:

With RS facing, 1dc in each of next 21 sts, make 7ch loosely, miss 25 sts (for sleeve), 1dc in each of next 20 sts, 2dc in next st, 1dc in each of next 19 sts (for back), make 7ch loosely, miss 25 sts, 1dc in each of next 21 sts.

Commence pattern:

Row 1: 1ch, 1dc in next st, miss 1 st, *[1tr, 2ch, 1tr, 2ch, 1tr] in next st, miss 1 st, 1dc in next st, miss 1 st; rep from * to last st, 1dc in last st.

Row 2: 4ch (for first tr and space), 1tr back in first st, *1dc in tr in centre of group from previous row, [1tr, 2ch, 1tr, 2ch, 1tr] in next dc; rep from * to last group, 1dc in tr in centre of group from previous row, [1tr, 2ch, 1tr] in last dc.

Row 3: 1ch, 1dc back in last tr from end of previous row, *[1tr, 2ch, 1tr, 2ch, 1tr] in next dc, 1dc in centre of group; rep from * to end, 1dc in second ch of 4-ch from previous row. Repeat Rows 2 and 3 of pattern until work

measures approx 36.5cm (14½in) from shoulder (or until required length).

Fasten off.

Sleeves (make two)

With RS facing, attach yarn to middle stitch of underarm.

Round 1: 3ch, 36tr evenly around armhole, ss in top of first 3-ch. (36 sts)

Round 2: 3ch, 1tr in each st to end, ss in top of first 3-ch.

Round 3: 2ch, 1dc in each st, ss in top of first 2-ch.

Round 4: Rep Round 3.

Fasten off.

Flowers

Using B and 3mm (D/3) hook, make 4ch, join with a ss in first ch to make a ring.

*3ch, 1tr in ring, 3ch, ss in ring; rep from * until 5 petals are made.

Fasten off. Using a yarn needle use loose end and weave around centre to make circle closed.

Using C, make a French knot in the centre, wrapping wool around needle 5 times.

Finishing

Sew back seam up to yoke using either backstitch or overstitch.

Attach flowers over the yoke join at front of dress.

Sew 3 buttons onto back of yoke to line up with holes in the treble stitches.

Sew in ends.

Toddler Dress

This is great as an overdress worn over leggings or thick tights. It has a pretty flared skirt and the buttons are crocheted using a fine cotton.

Materials

Rooster Almerino Baby
➜ 5 x 50g (1¾oz) balls – approx 625m (680yds) – of shade 509 Dolphin (blue) (A)

Anchor Aida 6-ply crochet cotton No.5
➜ 1 x 50g (1¾oz) ball – approx 200m (219yds) – of shade Navy (dark blue) (B)
➜ 2mm (B/1), 3.5mm (E/4), 4mm (F/5) and 5.5mm (I/9) crochet hooks
➜ 2m (80in) navy blue 1cm (½in) wide velvet ribbon

Abbreviations

ch chain(s); **dc** double crochet; **dc2tog** (double crochet 2 together decrease) insert hook in next st, yrh, pull yarn through (2 loops on hook). Without finishing st, insert hook in next st, yrh, pull yarn through (3 loops on hook), yrh, pull yarn through all 3 loops on hook; **htr** half treble; **rep** repeat; **RS** right side; **sp** space; **ss** slip stitch; **st(s)** stitch(es); **tr** treble; **yrh** yarn round hook

Special abbreviations

Picot 1 3ch, ss in first of 3ch, ss into same st as 3-ch, miss 1 st, ss in next st
Picot 2 3ch, [1dc, 3ch, 1dc] in next dc
V-st 1tr, 1ch, 1tr

Size

To fit age: 18–24:**24–36** months

Finished size

Chest	(cm):	55	60
	(in):	22	24
Length	(cm):	46.5	51.5
	(in):	18½	20½

Tension

5 patterns across x 3 patterns down over a 10cm (4in) square using a 4mm (F/5) hook.

Bodice

Using A and 4mm (F/5) hook, make
101:**109**ch.

Row 1: 1tr in fourth ch from hook, 1tr in each of next 3 ch, *1ch, miss next 3 ch, 3tr in next ch; rep from * to last 7 ch, 1ch, miss next 3 ch, 1tr in each of next 4 ch. 59:**64**cm (23⅛:**25⅛**in) across.

Row 2: 3ch (counts as 1tr) miss first tr, *1tr in each of next 3 tr, 1ch; rep from * to last 4 tr, 1tr in each of next 3 tr, 1tr in top of 3-ch from previous row.

Row 3: 3ch, miss 1tr, 1tr in each of next 3 tr, 1ch, 1tr in next tr, 1ch, miss next tr, *V-st in next ch sp, 1ch, miss next 3 tr; rep from * until last 6 tr, 1ch, miss 2 tr, 1tr in next tr, 1ch, 1tr in each of next 3 sts, 1tr in top of 3-ch from previous row.

Row 4: 3ch, miss 1tr, 1tr in each of next 3 tr, *1ch, miss next V-st, 3tr in next ch sp; rep from * to last ch sp, miss 1ch sp, 1ch, 1tr in each of next 3 tr, 1tr in top of 3-ch from previous row.

Rows 5–7: Rep Rows 2–4.

Divide for armhole, Front yoke:

Row 1: 3ch, miss 1tr, *1tr in each of next 3 tr, 1ch; rep from * 4:**5** times more ending with 1tr in last tr, turn (armhole side).

Row 2: 3ch, miss 4 tr, *V-st in next ch sp, 1ch; rep from * until 6 sts rem, 1ch, miss 2 tr, 1tr in next tr, 1ch, 1tr in each of next 3 tr, 1tr in top of 3-ch from previous row.

Row 3: 3ch, miss 1tr, 1tr in each of next 3 tr, 1ch, 3tr in next ch sp, *1ch, miss next V-st, 3tr in next ch sp; rep from * until 3:**4** groups are completed, ending with 1ch, miss next V-st, 1tr in top of 3-ch.

Row 4: 3ch, miss 1tr, 1ch, *1tr in each of next 3 tr, 1ch; rep from * once:**twice** more, 1tr in

each of next 2tr.

Row 5: 4ch, [V-st in next ch sp, 1ch] twice:**three** times, V-st in top of 3-ch.

Row 6: 3ch, [miss V-st, 3tr in next ch sp, 1ch] twice, V-st in next ch sp.

Row 7: 3ch, miss first tr, 1tr in each tr, 1ch over each ch sp, ending with 1tr in top of 3-ch.

Row 8: Rep Row 7.

Fasten off.

Back yoke:

With RS facing go back to last long row, miss next 4 sts for underarm, attach yarn in next tr.

Row 1: 3ch, *1tr in each of next 3 tr, 1ch; rep from * 10 times more, 1tr in next tr.

Row 2: 4ch, miss 4tr, *V-st in next ch sp, 1ch; rep from * to last 3 tr, miss 2 tr, 1tr in last tr.

Row 3: 3ch, 1tr in first ch sp, 1ch, *miss V-st, 3tr in next ch sp, 1ch; rep from * ending with 2tr in 4-ch sp.

Row 4: 3ch, miss first tr, 1tr in next tr, *1ch, 1tr

in each of next 3 tr; rep from * ending with 1ch, 1tr in last tr, 1tr in top of 3-ch.

Row 5: 4ch, miss 2 tr, *V-st in next ch sp, 1ch; rep from * ending with miss last tr, 1tr in top of 3-ch.

Rows 6–8: Rep Rows 3–5.

Fasten off.

Second front yoke:

With RS facing go back to last long row, miss next 4 sts for underarm, attach yarn in next tr.

Row 1: 3ch, *1tr in each of next 3 tr, 1ch; rep from * 4 times, 1tr in each of next 3 tr, 1tr in top of 3-ch.

Row 2: 3ch, miss 1 tr, 1tr in each of next 3 tr, 1ch, 1tr in next tr, 1ch, miss 2tr, *V-st in next ch sp, 1ch; rep from * three times, miss 3 tr, 1tr in top of 3-ch.

Row 3: 3ch, miss V-st, *3tr in next ch sp, 1ch; rep from * to last 4 tr, miss 1 tr, 1tr in each of next 3 tr, 1tr in top of 3-ch.

Row 4: Ss in each of first 6 sts, 3ch, 1tr in each of next 2 tr, *1tr in each of next 3 tr, 1ch; rep from * once more, 1tr in each of next 2 tr.

Row 5: 3ch, *V-st in first ch, 1ch; rep from * twice more, 1tr in top of 3-ch.

Row 6: 3ch, miss V-st, *3tr in next sp, 1ch, rep from * once more, 2tr in last 3-ch sp.

Row 7: 3ch, *1tr in each tr, 1ch over each ch; rep from * to end, 1tr in top of first 3-ch.

Row 8: Rep Row 7.

Fasten off.

Skirt

With RS facing, using A and 4mm (F/5) hook, join yarn in middle st of back bodice.

Round 1: 1ch, 1dc in same sp as ch, 1dc in each of next 4 sts, 2dc in next st, *1dc in each of next 5 sts, 2dc in next st; rep from * 6 times more, 1dc in each of next 11 sts, **2dc in next st, 1dc in each of next 5 sts; rep from ** 7 times more, 1dc in last st, ss in first dc.

Round 2: 5ch, *miss next dc, 1tr in next dc,

1ch; rep from * around to end, ss in fourth of 5-ch. (63 sts)

Round 3: 1ch, 1dc in same ch sp as ss, *1dc in next ch sp, 1dc in next tr; rep from * ending 1dc in last ch sp, join with a ss in first dc. (126 sts)

Round 4: 2ch, 1htr in next dc, *3ch, miss next dc, 1dc in next dc, 3ch, miss next 2 dc, 1htr in each of next 2 dc; rep from * ending last rep with 3ch, miss next dc, 1dc in next dc, 3ch, ss in top of first 2-ch.

Round 5: 2ch, 1htr in next htr, *3ch, [1dc, 3ch, 1dc] in next dc (picot 2 made), 3ch, miss next 3ch, picot 2 in next dc, 1htr in each of next 2 htr; rep from * ending last repeat 3ch, picot 2 in next dc, 3ch, join with a ss in top of 2-ch.

Round 6: 1ch, 1dc in same sp as ch, 1dc in next htr, 1dc in next ch sp, *5ch, miss 1 picot 2, 1dc in next ch sp, 1dc in each of next 2 htr, 1dc in next ch sp; rep from * ending with 5ch, 1dc in last ch sp, join with a ss in first dc.

Round 7: 1ch, 1dc in same sp as ch, 1dc in next dc, *miss 1dc, 7dc in 5-ch sp, miss next dc, 1dc in each of next 2 dc; rep from * ending with 7dc in last ch sp, join with a ss in first dc. (189 sts)

Round 8: 3ch (counts as 1tr), 1tr in next dc and in each dc around, join with ss in top of 3-ch. (189 sts)

Round 9: 1ch, 1dc in same sp as ch, 1dc in each tr, join with ss in first dc.

Change to 5.5mm (I/9) hook.

Round 10: 3ch, 1tr in next dc, *3ch, miss next 3 dc, 1dc in next dc, 3ch, miss next 3 dc, 1tr in each of next 2 dc; rep from * ending with 3ch, miss next 3 dc, 1dc in next dc, 3ch, join with a ss in top of 3-ch.

Round 11: 3ch, 1tr in next tr, * 3ch, [1dc, 3ch, 1dc] in next dc (picot 2 made). 3ch, miss next 3ch, picot 2 in next dc, 1tr in each of next 2 tr; rep from * ending last rep 3ch, picot 2 in next dc, 3ch, join with a ss in top of 2-ch.

Round 12: Rep Round 6.
Round 13: Rep Round 7.
Round 14: Rep Round 10.
Round 15: Rep Round 11.
Rounds 16–20: Rep Rounds 6–10.
Round 21: Rep Round 11, working tr instead of htr.
Round 22: Rep Round 6, making 7ch instead of 5ch.
Round 23: Rep Round 7, working 9dc instead of 7dc.
Round 24: 3ch, 1tr in next dc, * 4ch, miss next 4 dc, 1dc in next dc, 4ch, miss next 4 dc, 1tr in each of next 2 dc; rep from * ending with 4ch, miss next 4 dc, 1dc in next dc, 4ch, join with a ss in top of 3-ch.
Round 25: 3ch, 1tr in next tr, * 4ch, picot 2 in next dc, 4ch, miss next 4 ch, 1tr in each of next 2 tr; rep from * ending with 4ch, join with ss in top of 3-ch.
Round 26: Rep Round 6, making 7ch instead of 5ch.
Round 27: Rep Round 7, working 9dc instead of 7dc.
Rounds 28–31: Rep Rounds 24–27.
Round 32: Rep Round 8.
  Fasten off.

Sleeves (make two)
Using A and 4mm (F/5) hook, make 34ch.
Row 1: 2tr in fourth ch from hook, *1ch, miss next 2-ch, 3tr in next ch; rep from * to end. (11 tr groups)
Row 2: 3ch, miss 1tr, 1tr in each of next 2 tr, *1ch, 1tr in each of next 3 tr; rep from * ending 1ch, 1tr in each of last 2 tr, 1tr in top of 3-ch.

Shaping:
Row 1: Ss in each st to first ch sp, ss in first ch sp, 4ch, *V-st in next ch sp, 1ch; rep from * ending 1ch, 1tr in last ch sp. (8 V-sts)
Row 2: 3ch, 2tr in first ch sp, *1ch, miss V-st,

3tr in next ch sp; rep from * ending 1ch, 3tr in 4-ch sp.
Row 3: 3ch, miss 1tr, 1tr in each of next 2 tr, *1ch, 1tr in each of next 3 tr; rep from * ending 1ch, 1tr in each of last 2 tr, 1tr in top of 3-ch.
Row 4: 3ch, miss first 2 tr, V-st, 1ch in each ch sp, ending with 1tr in top of 3-ch.
Row 5: 3ch, miss first V-st, *3tr in next ch sp, 1ch; rep from * ending 1tr in top of 3-ch. (7 tr groups)
Row 6: 3tr, miss 1 group of 3 tr, *1tr in each of next 3 tr, 1ch; rep from * to last 3 tr group, miss last group, 1tr in top of 3-ch.
Row 7: 3ch, miss 1 st, 3tr, V-st, 1ch in each ch sp, ending with 1tr in top of 3-ch.
  Fasten off.

Buttons (make 4)
Using 2mm (B/1) hook and B, make 3ch, join with ss to form a ring.
Round 1: 1ch, 2dc in each ch, join with a ss in top of first 2-ch. (6 sts)
Round 2: 1ch, 2dc in each st, join with a ss in top of first 2-ch. (12 sts)
  Fasten off leaving a long tail, weave sts closed with a tapestry needle and pull tight.

Finishing
Sew sleeves in armholes.
Sleeve edging:
With RS facing and 3.5mm (E/4) hook, join yarn in st at seam.
  Picot 1 around, join with a ss in first 3-ch.
  Fasten off.
Armhole edging and front, back, side edgings:
With RS facing, and 3.5mm (E/4) hook, join yarn at top corner edge.
  1dc in each of next 11 sts to sleeve top, *dc2tog, 1dc in next st; rep from * across top of sleeve, back and second sleeve top,

finishing at top left front border.
  Fasten off.
  With RS facing and 3.5mm (E/4) hook, join yarn at base of right-hand front.
  1ch, make a picot edging using picot 1 around front, right-hand sleeve top, back, left-hand sleeve top and front up to end of front edging (not down straight edge of front).
  Sew buttons in place onto dress front.
  Weave ribbon in between spaces at waist, tie in a bow at the front.

CHAPTER FOUR

Toys, Accessories & Room Decorations

Honey Bunny

Honey Bunny is a pretty lilac rabbit with a cute dress. Made with beautifully soft yarn and safety eyes, she's just the right size to grip and cuddle.

Materials

Rabbit

Rooster Almerino Aran

➜ 1 x 50g (1¾oz) ball – approx 94m (103yds) – of shade 319 Lilac Sky (lilac) (A)

Rooster Baby Rooster

➜ Small amount of shade 502 Seashell (off white) (B)

➜ 5mm (H/8) crochet hook

➜ Small piece white felt

➜ Black safety eyes

➜ Small amount of black embroidery thread

➜ Fibrefill stuffing

Dress

Rooster Baby Rooster

➜ 1 x 50g (1¾oz) ball – approx 125m (136yds) – of shade 502 Seashell (off white) (B)

➜ Small amounts of shade 507 Urchin (pale pink) (C) and 504 Seaweed (green) (D)

➜ Scrap of shade 503 Sandcastle (yellow) (E)

➜ 3mm (D/3) crochet hook

Abbreviations

beg beginning; **ch** chain; **dc** double crochet; **dc2tog** (double crochet 2 together decrease) insert hook in next st, yrh, pull yarn through (2 loops on hook). Without finishing st, insert hook in next st, yrh, pull yarn through (3 loops on hook), yrh, pull yarn through all 3 loops on hook; **htr** half treble; **rep** repeat; **sp** space; **ss** slip stitch; **st(s)** stitch(es); **tr** treble; **yrh** yarn round hook

Special abbreviation

htr2tog (half treble 2 together decrease) *yrh, insert hook in next st, yrh, pull yarn through (3 loops on hook). Without finishing st, rep from * in next st (5 loops on hook), yrh, pull yarn through all 5 loops on hook

Finished size

Approx 25cm (10in) tall

Head

Using A and 5mm (H/8) hook, make 2ch, 4dc in second ch from hook. (4 sts)

Place st marker at beg of each round (when counting, loop on hook counts as one st).

Round 1: 2dc in each st. (8 sts)

Round 2: *1dc in next st, 2dc in next st; rep from * to end of round. (12 sts)

Rounds 3–4: 1dc in each st.

Round 5: *1dc in each of next 2 sts, 2dc in next st; rep from * to end of round. (16 sts)

Round 6: *1dc in each of next 3 sts, 2dc in next st; rep from * to end of round. (20 sts)

Rounds 7–9: 1dc in each st. (20 sts)

Round 10: *1dc in each of next 3 sts, dc2tog; rep from * to end of round. (16 sts)

Round 11: *1dc in each of next 2 sts, dc2tog; rep from * to end of round. (12 sts)

Cut two small white felt circles. Make a small hole in each centre, push safety eyes through felt and insert onto face. Stuff head.

EXPERT ADVICE

Use a stitch marker to mark the beginning and end of rounds.

Round 12: *1dc in next st, dc2tog; rep from * to end of round. (8 sts)

Round 13: Dc2tog around.
  Fasten off.

Body

Using A and 5mm (H/8) hook, make 2ch, 6dc in second ch from hook.

Round 1: 2dc in each st. (12 sts)

Round 2: *1dc in next st, 2dc in next st; rep from * to end of round. (18 sts)

Round 3: *1dc in each of next 2 sts, 2dc in next st; rep from * to end of round. (24 sts)

Round 4: *1dc in each of next 3 sts, 2dc in next st; rep from * to end of round. (30 sts)

Rounds 5–12: 1dc in each st.

Round 13: *1dc in each of next 3 sts, dc2tog; rep from * to end of round. (24 sts)

Round 14: *1dc in each of next 2 sts, dc2tog; rep from * to end of round. (18 sts)

Round 15: 1dc in each st.
  Stuff firmly.

Round 16: *1dc in next st, dc2tog; rep from * to end of round.

Round 17: *1dc, dc2tog; rep from * to end of round.
  Fasten off.

Ears (make 2)

Using A and 5mm (H/8) hook, make 2ch, 4dc in second ch from hook. (4 sts)

Round 1: *1dc in next st, 2dc in next st; rep once more. (6 sts)

Round 2: *1dc in next st, 2dc in next st; rep twice more. (9 sts)

Round 3: 1dc in each of next 4 sts, 2dc in next st, 1dc in each of next 3 sts, 2dc in last st. (11 sts)

Rounds 4–10: 1dc in each st.
  Fasten off.

Legs (make 2)

Using A and 5mm (H/8) hook, make 2ch, 6dc in second ch from hook.

Round 1: 2dc in each st. (12 sts)

Round 2: *1dc in each of next 2 sts, 2dc in next st; rep from * to end of round. (16 sts)

Rounds 3–4: 1dc in each st.

Round 5: *1dc in each of next 2 sts, dc2tog; rep from * to end of round. (12 sts)

Rounds 6–17: 1dc in each st.
  Fasten off.

Arms (make 2)

Using A and 5mm (H/8) hook, make 2ch, 6dc in second ch from hook.

Round 1: 2dc in each st. (12 sts)

Round 2: *1dc in each of next 2 sts, 2dc in next st; rep from * to end of round. (16 sts)

Rounds 3–4: 1dc in each st.

Round 5: *1dc in each of next 2 sts, dc2tog; rep from * to end of round. (12 sts)

Rounds 6–14: 1dc in each st.
  Fasten off.

Tail

Using B, make a small pompom by wrapping the yarn around two or three fingers approx 80 times. Gently slide the yarn off your fingers and tie a knot in the centre very securely. The pompom will now have loops on either side of the knot. Cut all the loops; trim and fluff the pompom into shape.

Making up

Pin and sew body to head. Make a running stitch around the outer edges to make the ears lie flat. Pinch ears at back and sew a slight fold. Pin and sew ears to head. Stuff legs and arms, pin and sew to body. Sew tail to body.

Dress

Using B and 3mm (D/3) hook, make 48ch, ss in first ch to form a ring.
  Place a stitch marker at beg of round.

Rounds 1–7: 1dc in each st. (48 sts)

Round 8: Htr2tog, 1htr in each st to end. (47 sts)

Round 9: Htr2tog, 1htr in each st to end. (46 sts)

Rounds 10–11: 1htr in each st to end. (46 sts)

Round 12: Htr2tog, 1htr in each st to end. (45 sts)

Round 13: 1htr in each st to end. (45 sts)

Round 14: Htr2tog, 1htr in each st to end. (44 sts)

Round 15: Htr2tog, 1htr in each st to middle of round, htr2tog (place stitch marker in dec stitch), 1htr in each st to end. (There should now be two stitch markers, one to indicate beg of round and one to indicate middle of round.) (42 sts)
  Fasten off.

Bottom of dress:
Turn dress upside down, join C to start of round.

Round 1: 1dc in each underside of first round of ch.

Round 2: *miss 1 st, 5tr in next st, miss 1 st, 1dc in next st; rep from * to end.
  Fasten off.

Left shoulder:
Turn dress right way up and work shoulder straps. With fasten off point on your right

(under the arm), join B in next st towards centre.

  1dc in next 3 sts.
  *1ch, 1dc in next 3 sts. (3 sts)
  1ch, 1dc in next 3 sts. (3 sts)
  1ch, dc2tog, 1dc. (2 sts)
  1ch, 1dc in next 2 sts. (2 sts)
  1ch, dc2tog. (1 st)
  1ch.
  1dc in ch. (1ch)
  2dc in ch. (2 sts)
  1ch, 1dc in each st. (2 sts)
  1ch, 2dc in next st, 1dc in next st. (3 sts)
  1ch 1dc in each 3 sts. (3 sts)
  1ch. 1dc in each of next 3 sts. (3 sts)
  Fasten off.

Right shoulder:
Join B on other side 4 sts from first strap.
  1dc in each of next 3 sts towards other arm.
  Rep from * of Left shoulder.

Neck edging:
  Using C, join yarn in ch where strap is narrowest.
  Make 6dc evenly down strap.
  1dc in next st, dc2tog in next st, 1dc in next st.
  Make 6dc evenly up neck side of other strap.
  Join with a ss in ch at top between front and back of strap (top of shoulder), 1ch, turn.
  1dc in next 15 sts around neck.
  Fasten off.

Finishing
Sew in ends.
  Stitch flowers around dress using D to embroider ch st and E to make French knots for centre of flower.
  Fit dress on Rabbit and hand sew straps in place at back of dress.

Coat Hangers

Show off your beautiful baby clothes on these cute hangers. They're much too nice to keep inside a wardrobe.

Materials

Watermelons

Rooster Almerino DK

→ 1 x 50g (1¾oz) ball – approx 112.5m (124yds) – each of shade 210 Custard (yellow) (A) and 207 Gooseberry (green) (B)

→ Small amounts of shade 220 Lighthouse (red) (C), 201 Cornish (off white) (D) and Rooster Baby shade 410 Liquorice (black) (E)

Chickens

Rooster Almerino DK

→ 1 x 50g (1¾oz) ball – approx 112.5m (124yds) – each of shade 207 Gooseberry (green) (F) and 208 Ocean (blue-green) (G)

→ Small amounts of 201 Cornish (off white) (H), Rooster Baby shade 411 Chocolate (brown) (I), 210 Custard (yellow) (J) and 220 Lighthouse (red) (K)

All hangers

→ 3.5mm (E/4) crochet hook

→ 35 x 20cm (14 x 8in) piece of wadding (for two hangers)

→ 2 wooden coat hangers

Abbreviations

ch chain; **dc** double crochet; **htr** half treble; **rep** repeat; **ss** slip stitch; **st(s)** stitch(es); **tr** treble; **yrh** yarn round hook

Special abbreviations

2ch picot 2ch ss into second ch from hook, pull tight

3ch picot 3ch, ss into third ch from hook, pull tight

trCl (treble cluster) *yrh, insert hook through ring, yrh, pull yarn through 2 loops (2 loops on hook); rep from * twice more (4 loops on hook), yrh, pull yarn through all 4 loops (1 treble cluster made)

Size

To fit hanger: approx 31cm (12½in) long

Finished size

Length: 31cm (12½in)

Cover (both hangers)

Using A or F, make 14ch.

Row 1: 3ch (counts as first tr), 1tr in fifth ch from hook, 1tr in each ch to end, turn.

Row 2: 3ch (counts as first tr), 1tr in each tr to last st, 1tr in top of previous 3-ch, turn.

Row 3: Rep Row 2 another 27 times or until work is long enough to cover coat hanger. Fasten off.

Small watermelon chunks (make 9)

Using C, 4ch, 2tr in first ch.

Fasten off.

Join in D, 1ch, 1dc in top of first tr, 2dc in second tr, 1dc in top of fourth ch.

Fasten off.

Join in B, 1ch, 2dc in each of next 4 sts.

Fasten off.

Using E, hand sew 3 sts on each chunk.

Watermelon large chunks (make 2)

Using C, 4ch, 1htr, 2tr, 1htr in first ch.

Fasten off.

Join in D, 1ch, 1dc in top of first st, 2dc into each of next 4 sts, ss into second of 4-ch from previous row. (9 sts)

Fasten off.

Join in B, miss 1 st, 2dc in each of next 8 sts. (16 sts)

Fasten off.

Using E, hand sew 3 sts on each chunk.

Large leaf (make 2 or more)

Using B, make 12ch.

Row 1: 1dc in third ch from hook, 1htr in next st, 1tr in each of next 6 sts, 1htr in next st, dc into end ch.

Row 2: 2ch, working down other side of base chains, 1dc into first st, 1htr in next st, 1tr in each of next 6 sts, 1htr in next st, 1ch, ss into next ch.

Fasten off.

Small leaf (make 18)

Using B, make 10ch,

Row 1: 1dc in third ch from hook, 1htr in next st, 1tr in each of next 4 sts, 1htr in next st, 1dc in end ch.

Row 2: 2ch, working down other side of base chains, 1dc in first st, 1htr in next st, 1tr in next 4 sts, 1htr in next st, 1ch, ss in next ch.

Fasten off.

Hens (make 3)

Using H, make 4ch.

Row 1: 5tr into first ch, turn.

Row 2: 3ch, 2tr in each of next 2 sts, 1tr in each of next 2 sts, 2tr in next st, 1tr in last st, turn.

Row 3: 3ch, 1dtr in first st, 1tr in next st, 1htr in next st, ss in each of next 4 sts, 2ch, 3ch picot, 1dtr in same st, 3ch picot, 1tr in next st, 3ch picot, 2ch, ss in last st.

Fasten off.

Rejoin yarn in top of htr on hen's head.

2ch, 1tr in each of next 2 sts, 2ch, ss into same st.

Fasten off.

Legs:

Using I and with RS facing, join yarn to middle of bottom edge of hen's body.

*3ch, [2ch picot] twice, ss in first ch of 2-ch; rep from * once more, ss back in bottom edge.

Fasten off.

Beak:

Join J to bottom of 2ch, 2ch picot.

Fasten off.

Under beak:

Join K to top of 3ch, 3ch picot.

Fasten off.

Comb:

Join K to top of head, [3ch picot] twice, ss in top of head.

Fasten off.

Chicks (make 6)

Using H, make 9ch.

Ss into sixth ch from hook, 1trCl into first ch, 3ch ss into first ch.

Fasten off.

Feet:

Using I and with RS facing, join yarn to middle of bottom edge of chick's body.

*4ch, ss into second ch, ss into first ch; rep from * once, ss back in bottom edge.

Fasten off.

Small flowers (make 2)

Make 4ch, join with ss to make a ring, 6dc in ring.

*Ss into first dc, 3ch, 1tr into same st, 3ch, ss into same st; rep from * five times. (6 petals)

Fasten off.

Finishing

Cover wooden part of coat hanger with a layer of wadding to pad.

Place crocheted cover around wadding and work dc to join along bottom edge. Fasten off.

Sew in ends on all crochet pieces.

Watermelon cover edging and hook embellishments

Join B to one end of bottom of coat hanger cover, make 4ch.

Put hook through middle of top of small watermelon chunk, pull yarn through and make fifth ch, make 4ch. Measure 3cm (1¼in) along bottom of hanger and join ch to cover with dc. Repeat to add remaining small chunks.

Fasten off.

Loops:

Using B, join yarn in work near base of hook. Make 30ch, ss back in work near hook, make 25ch, ss back in work near hook, make 27ch, ss back in work near hook.

Fasten off.

Leaves:

Place leaves at base of coat hanger hook and stitch in position. Stitch large watermelon chunks between leaves.

Sew in ends.

Chicken cover edging and hook embellishments

Using I, embroider eyes on hen and chicks. Join 1 hen, 3 chicks, 1 hen, 3 chicks, 1 hen together in order.

Join G to one end of bottom edge of coat hanger cover, ss through tail of hen, *make

12ch, ss through comb of same hen and back in base of coat hanger 6cm (2½in) from end of hanger. Make 8ch, ss in bottom edge of coat hanger cover approx 9cm (3½in) from end, make 8ch, ss in next hen tail and back in bottom edge of coat hanger cover; rep from * twice more.

Fasten off.

Leaves:

Place leaves at base of coat hanger hook and stitch in position, then place flowers on top of leaves around base of the coat hanger hook and stitch in position.

Sew in ends.

Happy Stars Cot Garland

This is a beautiful garland to hang in a baby's room. Drape it over the top of the cot for your baby to look at the beautiful colours and dangly flowers, or hang along the ceiling or wall.

Materials

Rooster Almerino Aran

➜ 1 x 50g (1¾oz) ball – approx 94m (103yds) – each of shade 318 Coral (orange) (MC), 307 Brighton Rock (bright pink), 315 Shimmer (pale grey), 316 Lagoon (blue) 317 Lolly (pale green), 319 Lilac Sky (lilac)

Rooster Almerino DK

➜ 1 x 50g (1¾oz) ball – approx 113m (124yds) – of shade 218 Starfish (bright orange),

➜ 4.5mm (G/6) and 3mm (D/3) crochet hooks

Abbreviations

ch chain; **dc** double crochet; **htr** half treble; **MC** main colour; **rep** repeat; **sp** space; **ss** slip stitch; **st(s)** stitch(es); **tr** treble

Finished size

Length: 142cm (56in) long

Stars (make 4 in each colour)

Using 4.5mm (G/6) hook, 6ch, join circle with ss in first ch.

Round 1: 1ch [1dc in circle, 3ch] 12 times, ss in first dc.

Round 2: Ss in each of next 2 ch, 1ch, 1dc in 3-ch sp from previous round [3ch, 1dc in next 3-ch sp] 11 times. 1ch, 1htr in top first dc.

Round 3: *6ch, 1dc in next 3-ch sp**, 3ch, 1dc in next 3-ch sp from previous round; rep from * 4 more times and from * to ** once more, 1ch, 1tr in htr that closed previous round.

Round 4: *[5tr, 2ch, 5tr] in next 6-ch sp, 1dc in next 3-ch sp; rep from * 5 more times, ending last rep in tr that closed previous round, ss in next st.

Fasten off.

Joining

Lay stars out in a row. Sew each star to the next one at the middle two points, using a yarn needle.

Using MC, make 50ch.

Do not fasten off.

With right side of garland facing and starting at the right-hand side, insert hook in middle space of top point of first star and make 1dc to join chain to star.

Make *15ch, 1dc in middle space of top point of next star; rep from * to last star, make 50ch for tie.

Fasten off.

Flowers (make 2 in each colour)

Using 3mm (D/3) hook, make 4ch, join with a ss to form a ring.

Make 5dc in ring, join with ss.

Ss in first st, *2ch, 1htr, 2ch, ss in same st, ss in next st; rep from * 4 more times.

Fasten off.

Finishing

Sew in ends.

Baby Cloths

These are handy and pretty little cloths to take around in your baby bag – so lovely you'll put everyone else's muslin cloths to shame. I adapted these traditional square patterns from vintage patterns found in my mother's craft drawer that were due for a well-earned airing.

Traditional square

Using A, make 4ch, join with ss to form a ring.

Round 1: 3ch (counts as first tr), 2tr in ring, 2ch, *3tr in ring, 2ch; rep from * twice; join with ss in first 3-ch.

Join B.

Round 2: Ss in first 2-ch sp, 3ch [1tr, 2ch, 3tr] in same ch sp, 1ch; *[3tr, 2ch, 3tr] in next ch sp (corner), 1ch; rep from * twice, 1tr in next ch sp, join with ss. (4 corners).

Join C.

Round 3: Ss in first 2-ch sp, 3ch [1tr, 2ch, 3tr] in same sp, 1ch, 3tr in next ch sp, 1ch, *[3tr, 2ch, 3tr] in next corner sp, 1ch, 3tr in next ch sp, 1ch; rep from * twice, 1tr in next ch sp; join with ss.

Alternate colours as set in each following row.

Rounds 4–8: Ss in first 2-ch sp, 3ch, [1tr, 2ch, 3tr] in same ch sp, 1ch, [3tr in next ch sp, 1ch] in each ch sp to corner, [3tr, 2ch, 3tr] in corner space; rep from * twice, 1tr in next ch sp; join with ss.

Fasten off.

Finishing

Sew in ends on wrong side. Block cloth.

Cassis (pink) (A), 239 Ice Water (light blue) (B) and 346 Atlantic (mid-blue) (C)

➔ 4.5mm (G/6) crochet hook

Abbreviations

ch chain; **dc** double crochet; **rep** repeat; **sp** space; **ss** slip stitch; **st(s)** stitch(es); **tr** treble

Finished size

22.5cm (9in) square

 Beginner

Traditional square

Materials

Rowan Handknit Cotton DK

➔ 1 x 50g (1¾oz) ball – approx 85m (93yd) – each of shade 351

Wave cloth

Materials

Rowan Handknit Cotton DK

→ 1 x 50g (1¾oz) ball – approx 85m (93yd) –
each of shade 334 Delphinium (lilac) (A),
352 Sea Foam (turquoise) (B), 351 Cassis
(pink) (C), 239 Ice Water (light blue) (D),
349 Ochre (yellow) (E) and 246 Atlantic
(mid blue) (F)

→ 4mm (F/5) crochet hook

Abbreviations

ch chain; **rep** repeat; **sp** space; **ss** slip stitch;
st(s) stitch(es); **tr** treble; **yrh** yarn round
hook

Special abbreviation

tr3tog (treble 3 together decrease) *yrh,
insert hook in next st, yrh, pull yarn through,
yrh, pull yarn through 2 loops on hook (2
loops on hook). Without finishing st, rep from
* in each of next 2 sts (4 loops on hook), yrh,
pull yarn through all 4 loops on hook

Finished size

22.5cm (9in) square

Wave cloth

Using A, make 33ch.

Row 1: 1tr in 2nd ch from hook, 1tr in next ch,
*1tr in each of next 3 ch, tr3tog over next 3
sts, 1tr in each of next 3-ch, 3tr in next ch; rep
from * ending last rep with 2tr in last ch.

Break yarn.

Row 2: Join B into first st, 2ch, 1tr in first st, *1tr
in each of next 3 sts, tr3tog over next 3 sts, 1tr
in each of next 3 sts, 3tr in next st; rep from *
ending last rep with 2tr in last ch. Fasten off.

Row 3: Join C into first st, 2ch, 1tr in first st,
*1tr in each of next 3 sts, tr3tog over next 3
sts, 1tr in each of next 3 sts, 3tr in next st; rep
from * ending last rep with 2tr in last ch.

Break yarn.

Work 15 rows of Row 2, changing colour
on each row.

Break yarn.

Finishing

Sew in ends on wrong side. Block cloth.

Floral Burst

Using A, make 6ch, join with ss in first ch to form a ring.

Round 1: 3ch (counts as first tr), 2tr in ring, 3ch, *3tr in ring, 3ch; rep from * 5 times more, join with ss in top of first 3-ch.

Round 2: With RS facing, join B, in any ch sp, 3ch, [2tr, 3ch, 3tr] in same ch sp, *[3tr, 3ch, 3tr] in next 3-ch sp; rep from * to end, join with ss in top of first 3-ch.

Round 3: Ss in each of next 2 sts, ss in next 3-ch sp, 3ch, 8tr in same ch sp, *[9tr in next 3-ch sp]; rep from * to end, join with ss in first ss.

Break yarn, do not fasten off.

Round 4: With RS facing, join C, 2ch (counts as first htr), 1htr in next st, 1dc in each of next 5 sts, 1htr in each of next 2tr, 1dtr in sp between next 3-tr groups on Round 2, *1htr in each of next 2 sts on Round 3, 1dc in each of next 5 sts, 1htr in each of next 2 sts, 1dtr in sp between next 3-tr groups on Round 2; rep from * to last st, 1htr, join with ss in first 2-ch.

Round 5: 3ch, 1tr in next htr, 1tr in next dc, 2tr in each of next 3dc, *[1tr in each of next 7 sts, 2tr in each of next 3dc]; rep from * ending 1tr in each of last 4 sts, join with ss in top of first 3-ch.

Round 6: 3ch, 3tr in next st, *1tr in each of next 12 sts, 3tr in next st;; rep from * to end, join with ss in top of first 3-ch.

Break yarn, but do not fasten off.

Round 7: Join D, 1ch, miss next st, 5tr in next st, miss next st, * [1dc in next st, miss next st, 5tr in next st, miss next st]; rep from * to end, join with ss in first dc.

Fasten off.

Finishing

Sew in ends. Block cloth.

Improver

Floral burst

Materials

Rowan Handknit Cotton DK

→ 1 x 50g (1¾oz) ball – approx 85m (93yd) – each of shades 309 Celery (green) (A), 351 Cassis (bright pink) (B), 353 Violet (purple) (C) and 263 Bleaded (off white) (D)

→ 4mm (F/5) crochet hook

Abbreviations

ch chain; **dc** double crochet; **htr** half treble; **rep** repeat; **RS** right side; **sp** space; **ss** slip stitch; **st(s)** stitch(es); **tr** treble

Finished size

22.5cm (9in) diameter

Enthusiast

Rose cloth

Materials

Rowan Handknit Cotton DK

→ 1 x 50g (1¾oz) ball – approx 85m (93yd) – each of shades 215 Rosso (red) (A), 351 Cassis (pink) (B), 334 Delphinium (lilac) (C) and 341 Mist (grey) (D)

→ 3mm (D/3) crochet hook

Abbreviations

ch chain; **dc** double crochet; **htr** half treble; **rep** repeat; **sp** space; **ss** slip stitch; **st(s)** stitch(es); **tr** treble

Finished size

22.5cm (9in) square

Rose cloth

Using A, make 4ch join with ss in first ch to form a ring.

Round 1: *2ch, 4tr in ring, ss in ring; rep from * 3 times more. (4 petals)

Round 2: Ss in back of second tr, (keeping yarn at back of work) *4ch, ss in base of second tr of next petal; rep from * twice more, 4ch, ss in ss from Round 1.

Round 3: [1ss, 5tr, 1ss] in each loop (4 petals), join with ss in first ss.

Drop loop, break yarn, but do not fasten off.

Round 4: Join B, *6ch, 1ss in back of ss between petals; rep from * 3 times more.

Round 5: 3ch (counts as 1tr), [2tr, 2ch, 3tr] in first loop, *1ch, [3tr, 2ch, 3tr] in next loop; rep from * twice more, ss in top of first 3-ch.

Fasten off.

Round 6: Join C in any corner sp, 3ch (counts as 1tr), [2tr, 2ch, 3tr] in same sp, *[1ch, 3tr] in each 1-ch sp to next corner, [1ch, 3tr, 2ch, 3tr] in next corner; rep from * to end, ss to top of first 3-ch.

Fasten off.

Round 7: Join D in any corner sp, 3ch (counts as 1tr), [2tr, 2ch, 3tr] in same sp, *[1ch, 3tr] in each 1-ch sp to next corner, [1ch, 3tr, 2ch, 3tr] in next corner; rep from * to end, ss to top of first 3-ch.

Fasten off.

Round 8: Join B in any corner sp, 3ch (counts as 1tr), [2tr, 2ch, 3tr] in same sp, *[1ch, 3tr] in each 1-ch sp to next corner, [1ch, 3tr, 2ch, 3tr] in next corner; rep from * to end, ss to top of first 3-ch.

Fasten off.

Round 9: Join C in any corner sp, 3ch (counts as 1tr), [2tr, 2ch, 3tr] in same sp, *[1ch, 3tr] in each 1ch sp to next corner, [1ch, 3tr, 2ch, 3tr] in next corner; rep from * to end, ss to top of first 3-ch.

Fasten off.

Round 10: Join D in any corner sp, 3ch (counts as 1tr), [2tr, 2ch, 3tr] in same sp, *[1ch, 3tr] in each 1-ch sp to next corner, [1ch, 3tr, 2ch, 3tr] in next corner; rep from * to end, ss to top of first 3-ch.

Fasten off.

Round 11: Join B in any corner sp, 3ch (counts as 1tr), [2tr, 2ch, 3tr] in same sp, *[1ch, 3tr] in each 1-ch sp to next corner, [1ch, 3tr, 2ch, 3tr] in next corner; rep from * to end, ss to top of first 3ch.

Fasten off.

Finishing

Sew in ends. Block cloth.

Billy the Bear

Billy is a happy bear made in rounds. He's very squidgy and easy to carry – don't over-stuff him, he should be lovely, soft and cuddly; break the stuffing into small pieces before inserting.

Materials

Rooster Almerino DK

→ 1 x 50g (1¾oz) ball – approx 112.5m (124yds) – each of shade 205 Glace (pale blue), 203 Strawberry Cream (pale pink), 208 Ocean (blue-green), 210 Custard (yellow), 220 Lighthouse (red), 201 Cornish (off white) and 207 Gooseberry (green)

→ 3.5mm (E/4) crochet hook

→ Black safety eyes

→ Fibrefill stuffing

→ Yarn sewing needle

→ Scrap of black yarn for face details

Abbreviations

ch chain; **dc** double crochet; **dc2tog** (double crochet 2 together decrease) insert hook in next st, yrh, pull yarn through (2 loops on hook). Without finishing st, insert hook in next st, yrh, pull yarn through (3 loops on hook), yrh, pull yarn through all 3 loops on hook; **rep** repeat; **RS** right side; **st(s)** stitch(es); **ss** slip stitch; **WS** wrong side; **yrh** yarn round hook

Finished size

Length: approx 34cm (13½in)

Tension

20 x 15 rows over a 10cm (4in) square working in double crochet using a 3.5mm (E/4) hook.

Head

Alternate colours every round, except for Rounds 1–2 and 25–26, which are the same.
  Using first colour, make 2ch.

Round 1: 6dc in second ch from hook. (6 sts)
  Place st marker at beg of each round (when counting, loop on hook counts as one st).

Round 2: 2dc in each st. (12 sts)
  Change colour on next and every following round.

Round 3: *1dc in first st, 2dc in next st; rep from * to end. (18 sts)

Rounds 4–5: 1dc in each st.

Round 6: *1dc in each of next 2 sts, 2dc in next st; rep from * to end. (24 sts)

Rounds 7–8: 1dc in each st. (24 sts)

Round 9: 1dc in each of next 7 sts, 2dc in each of next 10 sts, 1dc in each of next 7 sts. (34 sts)

Round 10: *1dc in next st, 2dc in next st; rep from * once more, 1dc in each of next 25 sts, 2dc in next st, 1dc in each of next 2 sts, 2dc in next st, 1dc. (38 sts)

Round 11: 1dc in each of next 11 sts, 2dc in next st, *1dc in each of next 2 sts, 2dc in next st, rep from * 4 times more, 1dc in each of next 11 sts. (44 sts)

Rounds 12–18: 1dc in each st. (44 sts)

Round 19: 1dc in next st, dc2tog, 1dc in each of next 2 sts, dc2tog, 1dc in each of next 30 sts, dc2tog, 1dc in next 2 sts, dc2tog, 1dc. (40 sts)

Round 20: 1dc in each of next 11 sts, dc2tog, 1dc in next 2 sts, dc2tog, 1dc in each of next 6 sts, dc2tog, 1dc in each of next 2 sts, dc2tog, 1dc in each of next 11 sts. (36 sts)

Round 21: 1dc in each st. (36 sts)

Round 22: *1dc in each of next 4 sts, dc2tog; rep from * to end. (30 sts)

Round 23: *1dc in each of next 3 sts, dc2tog; rep * to end. (24 sts)

Insert eyes in 9th row from nose and stuff head.

Round 24: *1dc in each of next 2 sts, dc2tog; rep * to end. (18 sts)

Round 25: *1dc in next st, dc2tog; rep from * to end. (12 sts)

Do not change colour.

Round 26: Dc2tog around. (6 sts)

Fasten off with a long tail approx 15cm (6in). Finish stuffing head then use yarn needle to thread tail through sts of last round to close gap neatly.

Sew in ends.

Ears (make 4)

Do not count loop on hook as one st on this section – st marker is not necessary.

Using off white only, make 2ch, 6dc in second ch from hook (do not join ring), turn. (6 sts)

Row 1: 1ch, 1dc in next st, 2dc in each of next 4 sts, 1dc in last st. (10 sts)

Row 2: 1ch, 2dc in first st, *1dc in next 2 sts, 2dc in next st; rep from * twice more. (14 sts)

Fasten off.

Join ears to head:

Place two ears with WS together, join yarn in one corner by pushing hook through both ears.

1ch, work 1dc around by pushing hook through both ears to join semi-circle top of ears. Ss in bottom corner of semi-circle to join.

Rep with other set of ears.

Fasten off. Sew ears onto head.

Body

Alternate colours every round, except for Rounds 1 and 2 and 30 and 31, which are the same.

Using first colour make 2ch.

Round 1: 6dc in second ch from hook, join round and each subsequent round with ss. (6 sts)

Round 2: 2dc in each st. (12 sts)

Change colour on next and every following round.

Round 3: *1dc in next st, 2dc in next st; rep from * to end. (18 sts)

Round 4: *1dc in each of next 2 sts, 2dc in next st; rep from * to end. (24 sts)

Rounds 5–7: 1dc in each st. (24 sts)

Round 8: 1dc in next st, 2dc in next st, *1dc in each of next 3 sts, 2dc in next st; rep from * to last 2 sts, 1dc in each st. (30 sts)

Rounds 9–10: 1dc in each st. (30 sts)

Round 11: *1dc in each of next 4 sts, 2dc in next st; rep from * to end. (36 sts)

Rounds 12–13: 1dc in each st (36 sts)

Round 14: *1dc in each of next 5 sts, 2dc in next st; rep from * to end. (42 sts)

Rounds 15–17: 1dc in each st. (42 sts)

Round 18: 1dc in each of next 8 sts, 2dc in next st, *1dc in each of next 4 sts, 2dc in next st; rep from * 4 more times, 1dc in each st to end. (48 sts)

Rounds 19–22: 1dc in each st. (48 sts)

Round 23: 1dc in each of next 3 sts, dc2tog, *1dc in each of next 6 sts, dc2tog; rep from * 4 times more, 1dc in each st to end. (42 sts)

Round 24: 1dc in each st. (42 sts)

Round 25: 1dc in each of next 4 sts, dc2tog, *1dc in each of next 9 sts, dc2tog; rep from * twice more, 1dc in each of next 3 sts. (38 sts)

Round 26: 1dc in each of next 3 sts, dc2tog, *1dc in each of next 8 sts, dc2tog; rep from * twice more, 1dc in each of next 3 sts. (34 sts)

Round 27: 1dc in each of next 3 sts, dc2tog, *1dc in each of next 7 sts, dc2tog; rep from * twice more, 1dc in each of next 2 sts. (30 sts)

Round 28: 1dc in each st. (30 sts)

Round 29: *1dc in each of next 3 sts, dc2tog; rep from * to end. (24 sts)

Stuff body.

Round 30: *1dc in each of next 2 sts, dc2tog; rep from * to end. (18 sts)

Do not change colour.

Round 31: *1dc in each of next st, dc2tog; rep from * to end. (12 sts)

Round 32: Dc2tog around. (6 sts)

Fasten off with a long tail approx 15cm (6in). Finish stuffing body and use yarn needle to thread tail through sts of last round to close gap neatly.

Legs (make two)

Round 1: 2ch, 6dc in second ch from hook.

Round 2: 2dc in each st. (12 sts)

Round 3: *2dc in first st, 1dc in next st; rep from * to end. (18 sts)

Round 4: *2dc in first st, 1dc in each of next 2 sts; rep from * to end. (24 sts)

Round 5–6: 1dc in each st. (24 sts)

Round 7: *Dc2tog, 1dc in next st; rep from * to end. (16 sts)

Round 8: 1dc in each st. (16 sts)

Rep Round 8 until work measures approx 12cm (4½in).

Fasten off.

Arms (make two)

Rep pattern as for legs.

Fasten off.

Finishing

Sew in ends.

Embroider nose and mouth detail. Pin pieces in place first to check positioning. Sew body to head with widest part at bottom. Stuff legs and arms and attach to body.

Suppliers

The yarns used in these projects should be available from your local yarn or craft store. If you can't find the correct yarn, try some of the websites listed here.

WEB SITES
Debbie Bliss
www.debbieblissonline.com

Coats Crafts Rowan Yarns
www.coatscrafts.co.uk

Purl Soho
www.purlsoho.com

Yarn Forward
www.yarnforward.com

Fyberspates
www.fyberspates.co.uk

Laughing Hens
www.laughinghens.com

UK STOCKISTS
Laughing Hens
(wool, hooks, accessories)
The Croft Stables
Station Lane
Great Barrow
Cheshire CH3 7JN
01829 740903
www.laughinghens.com

Fyberspates
Unit 6 Oxleaze Farm Workshops
Broughton Poggs
Filkins
Lechlade
Glos GL7 3RB
07540 656660
www.fyberspates.co.uk

Rooster Yarns
Laughing Hens online
Wool, patterns, knitting & crochet supplies
Online.
www.laughinghens.com
01829 740903

Rowan Yarns
Green Lane Mill
Holmfirth
West Yorkshire HD9 2DX
01484 681881
www.knitrowan.com

John Lewis
Stores nationwide
0845 604 9049
www.johnlewis.com

TUITION
Nicki Trench Workshops
Crochet, knitting, and craft workshops for all levels
Email: nicki@nickitrench.com

US STOCKISTS
Bluefaced Leicester
Wool2Dye4
6000-K Boonsboro Road
Coffee Crossing
Lynchburg
VA 24503
www.wool2dye4.com

Knitting Fever
Stockists of Debbie Bliss, Noro, and Sirdar yarns
www.knittingfever.com

The Knitting Garden
Stockists of Rowan yarns
www.theknittinggarden.com

Lets Knit
www.letsknit.com

WEBS
www.yarn.com

Yarn Market
www.yarnmarket.com

Unicorn Books and Crafts
www.unicornbooks.com

A.C. Moore
Stores nationwide
1-888-226-6673
www.acmoore.com

Crafts, etc.
Online store
1-800-888-0321
www.craftsetc.com

Hobby Lobby
Stores nationwide
www.hobbylobby.com

Jo-Ann Fabric and Craft Store
Stores nationwide
1-888-739-4120
www.joann.com

Michaels
Stores nationwide
1-800-642-4235
www.michaels.com

Index

anchor motif 39

baby cloths 118–21
baby shell cardigan 28–31
beanie hat 60–1
Billy the bear 122–5
blankets
   flower cot 76–7
   Ophelia buggy 64–5
   sweetheart 68–9
boat motif 60
bonnet, flower 72–3
bootees
   lilac 56–7
   star stitch 74–5
brimmed hat 62–3
buggy blanket, Ophelia 64–5
button bands 34
buttons 105

capes, petal 96–9
cardigans
   baby shell 28–31
   flower power 36–7
   frill-edged 44–7
   pocket trim 32–5
   pompom 42–3
   wrapover 22–5
chain 9
chain ring/circle 10
chain space 13
chick motifs 114
coat hangers 112–15
cot garland, happy stars 116–17

decreasing 14
double crochet 11
double crochet squares together 15
double crochet two stitches together 14
double treble 12
dresses
   pink baby 100–1
   toddler 102–5

fastening off 15
floral burst baby cloth 120
flower cot blanket 76–7
flower motifs 31, 37, 86–7, 91, 101, 114, 117
   blossoms 73
   hats 59, 63
   squares 76
flower power cardigan 36–7
frill-edged cardigan 44–7

half treble 11
half treble two stitches together 15
hats
   beanie 60–1
   brimmed 62–3
   flower bonnet 72–3
   pompom 70–1
   ribbon 58–9
heart motifs 40, 68
heart tank top 40–1
hen motifs 114
holding hook 8
holding yarn 9
honey bunny 108–11
hooded jacket 80–3
hook, holding 8

increasing 14
intarsia 13

jackets
   hooded 80–3
   toggle 92–5
joining new yarn 10
jumpers
   ship ahoy 38–9
   springtime 18–21
   strawberry kisses 48–53

leaf motifs 53, 114
lilac bootees 56–7
loop stitch 13

making rows 13
marking rounds 10
mittens, baby 66–7

Ophelia buggy blanket 64–5

petal cape 96–9
petal motifs 98
pocket trim cardigan 32–5
pompom cardigan 42–3
pompom hat 70–1
pompoms, making 65
ponchos 84–7
   tasselled baby 88–9

quadruple treble 12

ribbon hat 58–9
rose baby cloth 121
rows, making 13

shawls, blossom 90–1
ship ahoy jumper 38–9
slip knot 8
slip stitch 11
square baby cloth 118
squares, double crochet together 15
star stitch bootees 74–5
stars, cot garland 117
strawberry kisses jumper 48–53
strawberry motifs 53
stripy tank top 26–7

tank tops
   heart 40–1
   stripy 26–7
techniques 8–15
toddler dress 102–5
toggle jacket 92–5
toys
   bear 122–5
   bunny 108–11
   safety eyes 125
treble 12
triple treble 12

watermelon motif 113–14
wave baby cloth 119
wrapover cardigan 22–5

yarn
   holding 9
   joining 10
yarn around hook 9

Acknowledgements

My own babies are all grown up now and I don't have grandchildren yet, but I have really indulged in designing such a cute crochet book.

Making this book has been a real team effort and I'm privileged to have worked with such an enthusiastic and talented group of people. I'm indebted to my expert crocheters who helped enormously to get the projects finished in time: Carolyn Meggison, Sue Lumsden, Duriye Foley, Emma Lightfoot, Laura Ramage and Fran Wensel.

I've had enormous support from Andy Robinson and John Okell from Laughing Hens who supplied all the Rooster Yarns with such prompt and efficient service and who sent out to all the crocheters at a minute's notice.

Huge thanks also to Marie Clayton for her patience and expert editing and to Pat Cooper for stepping in and sorting out the pattern grading with prompt attention.

Thank you to all those at Cico Books for trusting me with yet another book project, especially to Cindy Richards, Pete Jorgensen and Sally Powell for putting together such a pretty book with incredible efficiency.

And the biggest thank you goes out to my amazing mother Beryl, for her hawk's eye at checking the patterns and diligence at working out patterns and crocheting like crazy to meet the deadlines and for her unquestioning support.